THE INSIDER'S GUIDE TO

AUSTRALIA

THE INSIDER'S GUIDE
JAPAN • CHINA • KOREA • HAWAII • HONG KONG • AUSTRALIA
THAILAND* • BALI* • MEXICO* • INDIA*

The Insider's Guide to Australia
First Published 1987
Reprinted 1988
Hunter Publishing Inc
300 Raritan Center Parkway
CN94, Edison, N.J. 08818
by arrangement with CFW Publications Ltd

© 1988 CFW Publications Ltd
Text ©1988 Child and Associates Publishing Pty Ltd

ISBN: 0 935161 65 1

Created, edited and produced by CFW Publications Ltd
130 Connaught Road C., Hong Kong
Editor in Chief: Allan Amsel
Design: Hon Bing-wah/Kinggraphic
Text and artwork composed and information updated
using Xerox Ventura software

All rights reserved. No part of this publication may be reproduced, stored in
a retrieval system, or transmitted in any form, or by any means,
electronic, mechanical, photocopying, recording, or
otherwise, without the written permission of the publisher.

In preparation

Printed in Korea

THE INSIDER'S GUIDE TO

AUSTRALIA

by Robert Wilson

HUNTER PUBLISHING, INC.
Edison, N.J.

Contents

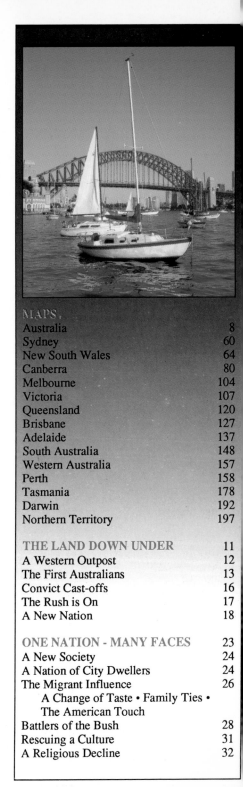

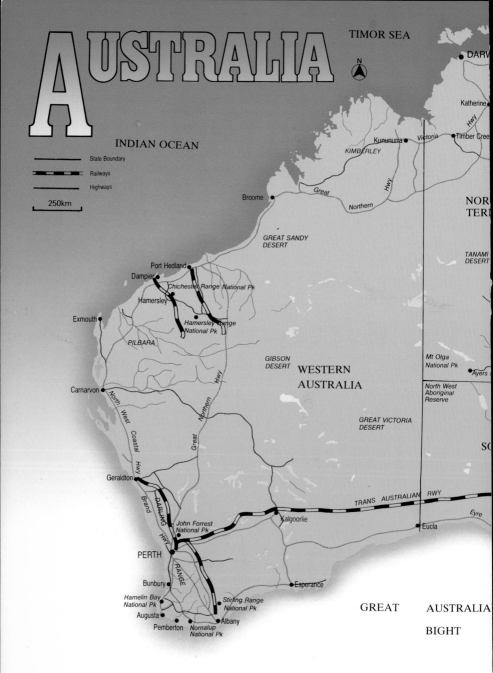

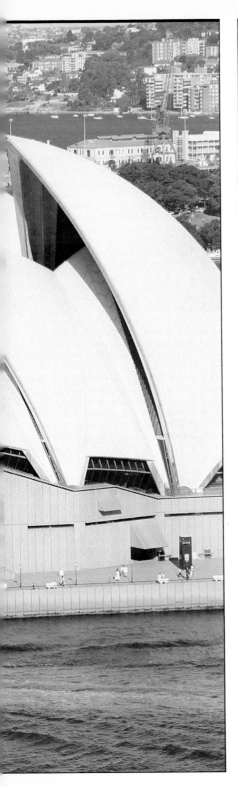

The Land Down Under

Australia is an anomaly. An English-speaking outpost of Western ways and values tacked on to the southern tail-end of Asia. Predominantly a vast, under-populated continent of wide open spaces just over the horizon from the teeming millions of Southeast Asia. A nation beyond the Indian and Pacific Oceans usually thought of as being the bottom of the world. It's Down Under - an expression, incidentally, reserved for foreign headline writers and rarely heard in Australia itself, least of all from Australians.

For centuries the continent was just a blur and a mystery in the minds of early European explorers. In some ways, it seems, things haven't changed all that much. Despite Australia's globally acclaimed achievements in many fields, and the fact that its minerals, energy and agricultural industries are some of the richest and most efficient in the world, the nation is still a question mark in many minds.

This widespread ignorance has spawned a number of myths and misunderstandings, most of which are exploded upon arrival. For example, the image of a wide sun-scorched land tended by a breed of tall, lean sheep farmers and cattlemen is, like most images, only part of the story. What is not generally known is that Australia is not a rural society at all; anything but. It is the most urbanized society in the world, with more than 70 per cent of the population jammed into its eight major cities.

Even a cursory look at a map tells you that Australia is big, but it is only when you get there that you begin to realize just how big. The vast empty spaces and what one writer termed "the tyranny of distance" only accentuates the sheer overpowering extent of Australia, the world's largest island and the driest of the continents.

It spans three - and sometimes four - time zones, and takes almost three days to cross by express train. Only five nations are bigger. Perth, in the west, is as close to Singapore as it is to Sydney, in the east. Highway One, the coastal road around the continent is almost as long as the distance from London to Honolulu. Western Australia is four times the size of Texas - or five times as large as France. Cattle stations in the Northern Territory are bigger than some American States.

Stretching from latitude 11 degrees

south on the tip of Cape York to the Roaring Forties regions of 44 degrees south of southern Tasmania, there are wide climatic variations. While the monsoon is drenching the humid tropical north between December and April, a dusting of snow may be falling on the mountain ranges behind Hobart. The northeast of Queensland is doused by 4,410 mm (174 in) of rain a year, while the huge arid Centre thinks itself fortunate to receive 250 mm (10 in) in the same period.

Despite the extremes of weather to be found across the continent, the climate along the eastern fringe where the vast majority of the 15 million Australians live, is most pleasant.

Seasonal differences are less noticeable the further north you go. Tasmania is chilled by winds from the polar region in winter and is coolish to warm in summer. Victoria is cold in winter, while winter in New South Wales is mild and both are delightfully warm to hot in summer. Queensland is hot most of the year, and you will find warm, balmy weather somewhere along the coast. It's advisable to stay away from the blistering heat of the center during the height of summer, and avoid the tropics during The Wet.

Adelaide in South Australia and Perth in the West both boast of their Mediterranean-like climates, and with a million people each are the only sizable centers of population away from the eastern seaboard and the farming-rich slopes and plains of the Great Dividing Range - the low mountain spine which runs down the entire coast. Sydney and Melbourne house half the people, which gives some explanation for the vast sprawl of those two cities.

In contrast, the dry and dusty Outback is virtually empty, with sheep and cattle stations needing immense tracts of semi-desert to support their stock. The Centre itself is thousands of square kilometers of inhospitality where one desert waste runs into another.

Yet the raw, unforgiving landscapes have their own primeval beauty, for Australia is the oldest of the continents, more than 3,000 million years in the making. The dramatic mesas and gorges of the ancient Kimberley and Hammersley Ranges in Western Australia are remains of a plateau which rose out of the oceans during the formation of the continent. Ayers Rock is sacred to the Aborigines, but its majesty also causes white visitors to feel its awesome presence.

To the eye the land looks hot and parched, but give it a sprinkling of rain and the desert blooms with hundreds of varieties of wildflowers. The magnificent coral of the Great Barrier Reef is the largest thing ever built by nature's organisms. Australia is truly a land of many wonders.

THE FIRST AUSTRALIANS

The Aboriginal culture and beliefs evolved from the land. The aborigines learned how to survive in even the harshest regions by gathering the offerings of nature.

Ancestors of the present-day Aborigines arrived at least 40,000 years ago. Anthropologists believe the first small groups could have come here as long ago as 150,000 years by island-hopping in large bamboo rafts southward from Southeast Asia and walking across the land-bridge which then connected New Guinea with northern Australia.

Early groups lived along the shores or rivers where food was plentiful, while those who followed moved inland where conditions were also habitable but much wetter than today. Lake Mungo in New South Wales, for instance, is a hot, dry stretch of earth which is a lake in name only; but up to 15,000 years ago it was a lagoon supporting a large population. Aborigines hunted and foraged only in the small communities that their lifestyle could maintain. They became highly adept and developed sophisticated ways of living with the land, the seasons and the animals on whom they were totally dependent for food, shelter and weapons. This finely tuned existence became the core of a complex culture which is the oldest living set of standards and beliefs in the world.

Cultural expression developed in the form of rituals based on dancing and art-derived forms with no written record. Traditions and stories have been passed on by word of mouth. Dream-time legends tell how the land was given to the

The features of this Arnhem Land Aborigine OPPOSITE and a drought scene in New South Wales OVERLEAF reflect the harsher side of Australia's climate.

people at the beginning of Time, when the Ancestral Beings rose from the earth in animal and human forms and created the landscapes as we see them now. After their work was completed the Beings returned to the rivers, water holes, trees, caves and rocks where they were born, the birthplaces remaining sacred and celebrated in ceremonies and song. This relationship continues even after death because Aborigines believe that when they die their spirits return to the sites from which they came.

It was this contrast in outlook toward the land - the Aborigine believing he is owned by the land and the European settlers concept of man owning land - that was to make the biggest impact on the estimated 300,000 Aborigines who inhabited the continent when the first Europeans arrived.

CONVICT CAST-OFFS

Australia was the last inhabitable land mass to be discovered. The continent was so large that early voyagers did not know what they had stumbled across and its discovery was preceded by a long history of accidents, near misses and sporadic exploration. The South Land, or New Holland, remained on maps for several centuries as an area drawing mostly on imagination and fantasy for its shape.

Chinese merchants may have touched its shores and fishermen from Indonesia certainly did. But it was left to the great maritime nations of Europe to put all the fragments of knowledge together. By the seventeenth century the Portuguese and Dutch were producing maps of the north and west coasts, but history had to wait until 1770 for Englishman James Cook to present an accurate account of the east coast and almost complete the picture.

The Dutch led the way with more than a century of exploration, but encountering only inhospitable shore and no signs of profitable metals or spices, they found no reason to lay claim to the land. Had they done so the history of Australia may have read very differently.

It was Cook, finding a coast far superior to anything the Dutch had seen, who planted his sovereign's colors.

England, however, found no use for its faraway possession until the American War of Independence deprived it of a place to send its convicts, and it was forced to find another dumping ground. Thus the First Fleet of 11 ships set out in 1787 for an unfriendly shore halfway around the world. The first years were extremely difficult, with the tiny colony locked in by the surrounding wilderness, starvation a constant danger, and labor in short supply because of the need for one half of the population to guard the other half. Punishment was harsh, and factionalism between the military and civilian authorities contributed to the colony's problems. Lethargy and inefficiency ruled.

It was almost 30 years before there was a significant expansion and movement of people, the conquest of the Blue Mountains opening up the fertile plains beyond. Following this breakthrough, explorers quickly spread out across the hinterland and along the rivers. Settlers, who with their flocks and herds were never far behind, laid claim to enormous tracts of land and became a major force. Within about 20 years settlements had become established at all of what are today's capital cities and the framework for the distribution of population set out.

Melbourne, Adelaide and Perth all managed to begin life without the help of convict labor, although Perth had later to bring in prisoners because of a slowdown in growth. As time went by, the number of free men who came to start a fresh life in this new land watered down the convict impact and brought a more normal and humane society. By the time transportation ended in 1868 in Western Australia, 157,000 convicts had been shipped from Britain; about half of this number going to New South Wales and 67,000 to Tasmania.

The transportation policy gave Australia two important assets, an administrative structure and a plentiful supply of labor, which if not always the most willing and healthy, was better than nothing. For many convicts, life was better in Australia than on prison hulks or in the old jails of England. While some convicts were hardened criminals who would make no contribution to the common good no matter where they were, many others were transported for less serious or even petty crimes and found stimulation in their new lives and went on to make valuable contributions to the development process.

THE RUSH IS ON

The face and mood of Australia changed forever in the 1850s, shortly after the California gold rush, with the discovery of gold in New South Wales and then, in prodigious amounts, in Victoria. The discoveries turned the economy and lifestyle of the colonies into a state of turmoil. Men abandoned the land and their jobs in the towns, and joined the latest gold rush. Crews jumped ship at the first port of call and headed for the diggings. Fortune-seekers came from all corners of the globe to join in the fever.

The goldfields were roisterous, untamed shanty towns peopled by hard workers and dreamers, villains and vagabonds. A few found fortunes, most remained poor. The few who wanted riches without working for them lived in the bush and subsisted on robbery with violence, earning the name "bush-rangers."

The upheaval was most marked in Victoria, where one strike followed another and old hands and newcomers alike chased the latest rumor to the newest field. In three years the gold-fevered population increased four-fold. The State today has more to show for those wealthy times than any of the other gold States, with the handsome

OPPOSITE A class of ceremonially dressed aboriginal children with their teacher in northern Queensland.

17

Gothic buildings that grace Melbourne, Ballarat and the other gold cities all paid for by profits from the goldfields.

The movement of people brought in by the gold strikes quickened contact between the colonies. The road network extended and railroads followed. Unfortunately each colony stubbornly took only its own considerations into account when deciding on a rail gauge, with the result that they each chose different widths and passengers were obliged to change trains at State borders. Even as late as the 1960s passengers between Sydney and Melbourne still had their journeys disrupted. Although a common gauge system has now been added to inter-capital routes, the nation is still paying an economic price for the early shortsightedness. Had the railroads been left to private enterprise, as in the United States, the problem probably would not have arisen.

Gold also forged a whole new mentality in the Australian people. The tens of thousands of new arrivals brought with them a global diversity of backgrounds, ideas and ambitions. They were people who expressed new thoughts and saw new horizons and visions. The concept of Australia being peopled almost exclusively by Anglo-Saxon stock who automatically turned to the Mother Country for succor and wisdom was beset on all sides.

Coinciding with the turbulence whipped up by the gold strikes was a shake-up in the power structure in the eastern colonies where the power, the people and the purse resided. Since the arrival of the First Fleet all management over the eastern half of the continent had rested in Sydney. But with their growth and new-found wealth, the settlements of Melbourne and Brisbane were becoming restless. Why, they argued, should they not become their own masters?

Brisbane had long since ceased to be a penal outpost and explorers and settlers had pushed far inland to discover the potential pastoral wealth. Isolation from the Sydney decision-makers and impatience with the administrative delays that distance made inevitable caused the farming squatters and town-dwellers alike to feel neglected.

Similar sentiments were echoed in Melbourne where the community became angry because the Sydney authorities were using Victoria's revenue for the betterment of Sydney.

Agitation and increasingly strong voices eventually brought separate colonial status to Victoria in 1851 and to Queensland eight years later, the agreements defining the interstate boundaries which exist today. As the nineteenth century progressed the remaining habitable land was settled and developed. With the help of large-scale land clearance, the development of the railroad system, the invention of refrigeration and the introduction of irrigation, Australia laid the foundations for what has become an agricultural economy of world standing. Australia's wool, wheat, beef, sheep and fruit are now bywords in excellence on international markets.

A NEW NATION

Since their earliest days the colonies have arrived at informal agreements when it suited them, trade and profit usually being the common factors which overcame the jealousies and rivalries that were never far from the surface. But such a fractured, self-seeking system could not continue to exist in an expanding world where international commerce was becoming more complex, and throughout the 1880s there was a growing realization that some form of federation between the squabbling colonies was essential for the future welfare of the continent as a whole. It was however, to be a long and difficult birth spread over decades before Australia

was to emerge as a nation.

Each colony had its own priorities and worries. New South Wales, which was increasingly seen as a leader, felt its free trade policy would be jeopardized; Queensland resisted because its Pacific native labor in the cane fields was against the federalists' all-white policy; thinly-populated Western Australia feared it would be dominated by the more populous States.

Inter colonial distrust and the refusal of New South Wales to take part were responsible for wrecking a conference in 1883. But a more successful meeting eight years later did agree on the basic form for the Federal Government and sharing of authority as it exists today; with a House of Representatives lower house elected by districts and decided on a population basis, a Senate upper house of review consisting of an equal number of members from each State, a separate judiciary, and an Executive consisting of the Governor-General, as the monarch's representative, and his advisers.

Now came the long and arduous task of selling federation to the colonial governments and the people, and it took another nine years before the people of all the colonies had voted for the creation of the Commonwealth of Australia. It was an eventual triumph of patience, tolerance, compromise and sheer hard work, yet opponents voiced their doubts to the end.

While all this was going on, the British government in London was watching events very closely to ensure that its interests and investments were protected. The constitution, when finally thrashed out, kept Australia's ties with Britain as strong as ever; firstly because the colonies still trusted London more than they trusted one another, and secondly because England wanted it that way, with Australia remaining inside the imperial sphere of influence. It was to be a white, liberal democracy.

So Australia began the new century with a hurrah of hope and optimism, being finally bestowed with nationhood on January 1 1901. A new century, a new beginning.

Unfortunately it was to be blood and carnage which gave Australia its first important emotional cohesion as a nation. As part of the Empire, Australia automatically went to war against Germany in 1914, and she was to find glory in disaster. In the crushing defeat inflicted by the Turks on the Allied landing force at Gallipoli, Australia suffered more than 8,000 dead, but heroes and tales of glory rose out of the massive blood-letting.

On the battlefields of France Australia lost thousands more of her young men - the generation that was supposed to build up a new nation - and suffered a higher proportion of casualties than any of the Allies. These campaigns forged the reputation of the Australian fighting man as a formidable warrior, a distinction en-

Sandhurst (Bendigo) as it appeared in 1857, the gold rush period. Illustration by S. T. Gill from *Victoria Illustrated*, first published in 1857.

dorsed 30 years later in the deserts of North Africa and jungles of the Pacific.

Along with so many other countries, Australia's fortunes slumped between the wars under the burden of low export prices and the Depression; but she came out of the cauldron of the second conflict in many ways changed and in many ways the same. The nation was unified, with a more confident outlook. Wartime needs boosted heavy industry and manufacturing, the many American troops demonstrated a different way of life and standard of technology, self-reliance was more in evidence, and Australia had become a dominant power in her corner of the world.

But many prewar attitudes were unchanged. With mass air travel a thing of the future, Australia was still isolated. So Australians picked up the pieces and went about business as before, a nation of conforming conservatives with a strong British background and an allwhite policy to ensure that the insularity was not sullied by any foreign inbreeding.

But all that was to change. Following the misery of the Depression in the '30s, expansion during the war had revived optimism about an industrial future, with the result that as the War drew to a close support grew for large-scale immigration. A home market would be needed for the expected rapid growth of goods and services, and workers would be needed to meet the labor shortage.

In addition, Australia was feeling vulnerable in the aftermath of the war. Darwin had been bombed, Japanese midget submarines had entered Sydney Harbour and Japanese forces had come perilously close to the nation's shores, being halted at the eleventh hour only after a fierce campaign in the jungles of New Guinea. So the old catch cry "Populate or Perish" was heard again to support the view that a population of a least 25 million was vital for the nation's security.

Meanwhile, on the other side of the world, millions of people in war-torn Europe were looking for a new and happier life. In gloomy, depressed Britain, where rationing persisted and the country was slow to get back on its feet, people thought they deserved something better for winning the war. In Europe, millions of displaced persons and refugees languished in camps, waiting desperately for a chance to build a new future.

So the mass exodus was organized; an immense movement of people which saw more than two and a half million new Australians enter the country between the end of the war and 1970. Boatload after boatload of them arrived, speaking many languages and coming from a multitude of backgrounds. Almost half were of British stock, lured by cheap passages, promises of good wages, and posters showing pictures of sunshine and golden beaches. Large numbers also came from the Mediterranean countries (as a result, Melbourne now has the largest Greek population of any city outside Athens). Many of the thousands of displaced persons who migrated came from the ravaged countries of northern and central Europe.

The immigrants brought with them a cultural heterogeneity and a new vitality to a previously parochial Australia. They took the "dirty jobs" when necessary, and also entered every sphere of professional and artistic endeavor. The result of this huge influx is that postwar migrants and their Australian-born children today account for 25 per cent of the population.

During the 1960s Australia enjoyed a period of unprecedented prosperity. There was a ready market for all her agricultural products; the discovery of oil in the Bass Strait made her almost self-sufficient; the development of iron ore deposits in Western Australia went hand-in-hand with lucrative contracts with Japanese steel companies; huge coalfields were expanded; the discovery of large deposits of uranium and bauxite

was a bonus; the burgeoning population ensured manufacturing prosperity.

The 1970s saw the first signs of a hiccup in the good times, a process which has accelerated into the present decade as the global growth in economy has slowed down. World over-production and the creation of the European Common Market, particularly with the entry of Britain, has either made markets for agricultural products more difficult to hold, or closed them altogether.

A slowdown in steel production has been felt in iron ore mines. The large coalfields of New South Wales and Queensland have made Australia the world's largest coal exporter, but buyers are demanding more competitive prices. Oil reserves are dwindling. Manufacturing has dropped away alarmingly in the face of cheaper imports. Unemployment has risen, and so has inflation.

Apportioning the blame depends on whom you talk to. Employers blame higher wages, workers blame poor management and the lack of investment. Certainly the amount spent on research and development is low compared with other developed countries.

Australia has learned at her cost that it is no longer possible to meet the bills and pay the national way by merely digging up another mineral mountain and shipping it overseas, or growing more crops in the hope that there will be a foreign buyer. The nation must decide quickly whether she is prepared to invest in herself and attempt to catch up in terms of modern technology and competitiveness.

ABOVE Army cadets marching on Anzac Day, April 25, the day when Australia honors its war dead.

One Nation – Many Faces

A NEW SOCIETY

The culture of Australia is very much a force in the making. Although two hundred years of immigration from Europe have all but drowned the culture of the Australian Aborigines, its significance has gained attention and is an important strand among many others that have been brought to Australia in the ethnic diversity of immigrants from all over the globe. The result is not yet a new Australian cultural identity but rather a cultural awakening which the visitor can observe in every area of the visual and performing arts.

The ethnic diversity, a product of a more recent wave of immigration, has made Australia a more colorful society. The establishment is British, down to its bewigged judiciary and symbolic mace in Parliament. But overlaid upon this foundation, layer upon layer, are the multi-national attitudes brought with them by new Australians from Europe and latterly from Asia, and the powerful imported influences of the United States. Cultures are living things, constantly changing through the absorption of new factors. Australia's culture has in the last few years evolved more quickly than most.

A NATION OF CITY DWELLERS

One of the puzzles when discussing the different aspects of Australia's ethnic identity is deciding which is the "real" Australia.

Is it the Australia of the sweeping plains and of the huge flocks of sheep tended by sturdy ruddy-faced men of the land sitting on their stock horses. This is the picture which symbolizes Australia overseas, the Australia of the travel poster and the one enshrined in numerous novels.

Or is the "real" Australia typified by the comfortable, variegated lifestyles of the cities, in which seven out of ten live, far removed from the rigors of a rural life? One of the nation's paradoxes is that despite its space, such a large proportion crowd into the big cities, making Australia the most urbanized country in the world. About 50 per cent of the population live in the sprawling cities of Melbourne and Sydney. In contrast, only 140,000 people populate the vast area of the Northern Territory.

Australians have always clung together in this fashion. In the beginning it was for protection and the need for combined endeavors to tame a forbidding country in which lay little beauty or assets, and to ward off the Aborigines.

Later, with all the colonies established on the coast and the beginnings of centers of population that could support themselves, it naturally followed that newcomers ventured little further than their port of landing; a situation which accelerated and fed upon itself the larger the cities became. Once the best farming land was settled and the rural community had sufficient hands to tend the land and provide all the services, there was little incentive or need for others to give up an existence on the salubrious coast for the rigors of the country. It has always needed something like a gold rush, jobs created by a large mineral discovery or even the foundation of a national capital to attract people inland.

Apart from Canberra, Ballarat and Bendigo in Victoria and Toowoomba on Queensland's Darling Downs are the only cities away from the coast with more than 50,000 residents. And all four, while physically inland, are hardly Outback centers of population, all being less than a two-hour drive from the coast.

This heightened herd instinct has brought about cities which stretch endlessly from one anonymous suburb into

OPPOSITE Wave-worn columns at sunset off the Victorian coast.

the next and typify the nation's post-war growth. Fly into any city and you glide in over rank upon rank of tightly-packed red roofs, with the occasional sparkle of a backyard pool to break the neat pattern. The sight symbolizes the Great Australian Dream of owning your own single-story free-standing brick cottage set in its own garden.

The Dream has come true to such an extent that almost three-quarters of Australia's five million homes are owned or in the process of being bought by their occupants, giving Australia the world's highest proportion of home ownership.

These urbanites rarely venture far out into the country, despite their cars and mobility. It is a constant lament of farmers and people in the country, especially during droughts and other hard times, that the city folk don't understand or appreciate the problems of their country cousins.

This reluctance to leave the city and travel afar is to a large extent a matter of time and distance. It is a hardy family who will contemplate a holiday or expedition that entails driving hundreds of kilometers along a road system which is improving only slowly, with a bunch of restless children in the back seat. As a result, a large proportion of long-distance travelers in Australia today are those who have retired and find themselves with the time and freedom to see their own country for the first time.

THE MIGRANT INFLUENCE

A CHANGE OF TASTE

The first migrants to Australia - eleven free settlers - arrived only a few years after the beginning of white settlement.

Every aspect of contemporary Australian life is influenced by the immigrant influx which followed, culminating in the surge of almost three million

arrivals following World War II. They have made their presence felt in new attitudes and values, in new ideas and horizons in ways big and small.

One of the first signs of a new nationality settling in Australia is in the restaurant business, eateries often starting in humble premises and then moving up-market. Trendy Australians are adventurous when it comes to dining out, and they are prepared to try anything at least once. The fact that the newest vogues may be Lebanese and Vietnamese might indicate the countries from which Australia has been receiving her most recent migrants.

But the stamp of the migrant goes deeper than the pleasures of the table. New Australians have found unexploited riches in the economy especially in service industries, light engineering and building; and in enterprises such as corner stores and grocery businesses which entail working long hours but can involve the family.

Newcomers have widened Australian perceptions in other directions as well. They not only brought new skills and

influence has served to make Australian life less conservative and watered down the three-piece-suit mentality prevalent for so long.

FAMILY TIES

Two-thirds of the southern European migrants came to this country through chain migration, by which early arrivals encouraged family members and friends to follow. Some chains eventually brought out hundreds from the same village or district, resulting in many close-knit national enclaves. Greeks have concentrated in Marrickville in Sydney, Lygon Street in Melbourne is dubbed "Little Italy" and thousands more Italians live in neighboring suburbs. Slavs have also banded together, while British are most evident in Perth and Adelaide.

This clustering together preserved a sense of continuity and interdependence in the transition to a new way of life, in some places it appears that Australia changes more than the migrants. Those from southern European backgrounds remain particularly close. Go to any park or beach on a sunny day and you will find the largest group is almost invariably of Mediterranean stock, with the men playing cards or dominoes while the women prepare the food and care for the children.

So tight knit are some immigrant communities that it is estimated that a million Australians cannot speak English, but such marked contrasts, however, do not extend beyond the first generation as children quickly conform to Australian ways and become Australians on the surface, taking many of their peers, attitudes, values and customs.

Although immigrants have settled mostly in towns, significant numbers have chosen to live in rural areas and been instrumental in setting up entire in-

fashions; they also swelled the interest in music, painting and other arts as well as the appreciation of good wine.

Academics and professional people were in many cases singled out for particularly harsh treatment in occupied countries during World War II and in the post-war period they were as eager as anyone else to find a new home in which they would be able to express themselves and exercise their minds. Not only did Australia bring in boatloads of budding shopkeepers or fruit-growers; she also welcomed new intellects.

All these newly-introduced social influences from abroad also brought a welcome informality into Australian life and softened the sometimes stolid and stuffy conformity of the "British way of doing things" that had been the norm. This disdain for convention expressed itself on occasions, in seemingly insignificant ways - migrants from warm climates knew better than to wear serge suits through the heat of summer, or to sit down to a steaming, heavy dinner in the noon of a hot Christmas Day! Their

Opal miners OPPOSITE in Coober Pedy and an aborigine station hand ABOVE at work in the Outback

dustries, some going back several generations.

The most conspicuous example is the Barossa Valley in South Australia, settled 130 years ago by German Lutherans fleeing persecution. Here, the ways and traditions of the homeland are still cherished and very evident. In similar fashion, a few kilometers away on the Eyre Peninsula the character of Cornish miners lives on in old tin towns.

Italians and Greeks who brought farming skills and experience from their homelands have been invaluable in de-

veloping orchards and vineyards. Maltese and Yugoslavs are heavily involved in market gardening, and there is even a community of Sikhs among the banana plantations of northern New South Wales. In the 1920s when the United States imposed immigration laws, the first Italian families moved into the sugar cane areas of northern Queensland and now dominate farming in that region.

THE AMERICAN TOUCH

The thousands of American soldiers stationed in Australia during World War II did much to turn Australian eyes increasingly away from Britain and across the Pacific toward the United States.

American influence has increased

ABOVE German influence in the Barossa Valley. OPPOSITE Elegant Victorian era iron lace curtains a Sydney terrace.

markedly since the War. Now when children go out for a treat, they want to go to McDonald's or Kentucky Fried, washing down their hamburger or chicken with a Coke or milk shake. Ten-pin bowling alleys have their leagues, jargon and devotees, and drive-in cinemas flicker in the suburban night. Australia has also gone through jitter-bugging, hula-hoops, pinball machines and other imported fads from across the ocean.

With the electronic global village upon us, television viewers can tune into a "live" news and current affairs program from New York, while Australian youth discos to American pop sounds as well as their home-grown versions.

BATTLERS OF THE BUSH

Leave the cities and enter the Outback or bush, and the difference extends to more than just the view; there is also the contrast in viewpoint. The wit can be as dry as the dust in the street outside the pub, and the philosophy 'things will probably get bloody worse, if that's bloody possible, but they could get better, although don't bloody rely on it.'

It's a wisdom born out of the experience that bad years are more likely than good, and any period of prosperity will be temporary and followed by drought, flood, bush-fire, pestilence and any other imaginable calamity.

The outlook might out of long habit lean toward the gloomy side, but it is not one of complete discouragement because there is the unspoken certainties that comes from knowing that the rest of Australia needs the interior more than the interior needs the city. After all, the nation lived off almost nothing more then the sheep's back until coal and ore exports came along.

Social life in the bush revolves around the traditional institution of the pub. It's the information office you go

is, it's the bank if you want to borrow a couple of dollars, it's the committee room when it comes to organizing an outing. And it's here a visitor will hear the yarns and tall tales from characters of doubtful age whom the folks back home will never believe.

Walk into a country pub and the locals will cautiously look you over and then go about their business, leaving you to make the first move. You can be as friendly or as withdrawn as you wish, but country folk like nothing better than to yarn with a stranger. A remark about the crops or the weather is often sufficient to strike up a casual conversation, and before you know it you could find yourself in a "school" of company, and taking your turn to buy the group you are with a round of drinks, usually raucously expressed as "it's my shout" with a call to the bartender to do the necessary filling of glasses. After observing this vital social grace your acceptance will be complete.

The big day on the bush calendar is the local show, and rare indeed is the township without its show ground. It's the social highlight, and in the more remote areas of the Outback families will

drive hundreds of kilometers over dirt roads to make sure they don't miss the occasion. It's a chance to meet the neighbors and catch up with the gossip.

The show ring is a non-stop procession of cattle and sheep being judged; the women drop in at the competition tent and enter their handicrafts and jars of preserves; the men-folk congregate around the beer tent and re-shape the world; the young folk flirt and promise to meet at the bush dance later in the evening. It's a scene familiar to rural life the world over.

The gradual improvement of bush roads and the advent of the motel have brought town and country closer together. The introduction of long-service leave as a part of general work conditions has given more urban dwellers the time and opportunity to see their own country, and tourism has brought new dollars into the country towns. This in turn has spurred rural pride in the form of museums, festivals and other ways of showing off the heritage of the bush. Alice Springs is a prime example of how tourism can change the Outback. Two decades ago it was a quiet cow town; today it is a town with a bustling casino and shiny-roofed suburbs.

This breakdown of barriers has improved country living considerably. Air-conditioning and modern appliances have brought more domestic comfort and made the dust and flies less trying; radios bring the world into the living room; and now, thanks to satellites, even the most remote Outback homestead can receive television.

Yet traditions and pride in the bush remain a strength of the national character, even among the city folk who are not always aware of it. Waltzing Matilda, a bush ballad, is Australia's unofficial national anthem the world over; the works of bush poets and writers, such as "Banjo" Paterson and Henry Lawson, are best-sellers when republished; a television serial about life in a country own constantly tops the ratings; and two other programs reflecting country life continue to run year after year.

RESCUING A CULTURE

Before Australia was forever changed by the rude arrival of European settlers, it was populated by nomadic Aborigines. While this society was in fact well developed, with rudimentary skills in making weapons and instruments and an intense and complex religious life animated with music and dance, the early European settlers rode rough-shod over the land rights of the Aborigines in the belief that they had none because they had done nothing to develop the land. As nomads they had no settled habitations to which they could later be granted title, as in the case of American Indians, and their society was so fractured and scattered that they did not have the political organization to coordinate any resistance against white men.

When Governor Phillip landed with his soldiers and convicts it is estimated that 300,000 Aborigines lived across the continent; the population now is probably half that number in varying degrees of assimilation. Many are located in northern Australia, and two-thirds live in cities.

Efforts have been made within the last 20 years to redress the injustices, but it is a long and complex process beset by problems such as poor education and housing, poverty, lack of work and resentment against the white man. As a result, most Aborigines remain poor and are the single most disadvantaged group in the nation.

Advances are being made, however, and cultural pride is being restored in many quarters despite setbacks and occasional outbreaks of racial violence.

New laws in the 1960s gave overall control of Aboriginal affairs to the Federal government, and Aborigines were given the right to vote. Increased and coordinated expenditure on health and housing has begun to show results, and organizations established by governments and Aborigines themselves have created a forum for opinion and gone part of the way to meeting the important demand for self-management.

Legislation concerning land rights, the most critical issue, now gives Aboriginal groups the legal framework to lay claim to inalienable Crown land on the ground of traditional significance. This has led to increasing conflict with mining companies, particularly in Western Australia.

Vast areas of Outback, including Arnhem Land and much of Northern Territory, are Aboriginal reserves, with permission of entry required for non-Aborigines.

In the north there has been a move out of missions, settlements and reserves back to out-stations in the traditional homelands where extended family groups

Contrasts. OPPOSITE Victoriana and Sydney's Centrepoint Tower, Australia's highest structure BELOW. In Perth, mock-Tudor in London Court and a highrise.

can live without the influence of other cultures. This in turn has encouraged a resurgence of the traditional lifestyle and social organization. Some groups have been able to set up their own business, such as a cattle station, with official guidance. Similarly, part of the education process for whites has been an increased awareness and appreciation of Aboriginal arts and skills.

However, much remains to be done and it is a long trek back to the homelands and the former ways for Aborigines intent on rescuing their unique culture.

A RELIGIOUS DECLINE

Fewer Australians are going to church, and census figures show an accelerating fall in organized religion which concerns almost every denomination. At the same time the number of people professing their "disbelief" has risen phenomenally.

The two most prominent Churches, the Church of England and the Roman Catholic Church, have both suffered. The Church of England has always been the largest denomination, but it never be-

came the "established" Church as it did in England and its numbers have fallen dramatically to less than 30 per cent of the total number of church goers. It is now only slightly ahead of the Roman Catholic Church whose numbers rose considerably due to immigration from European Catholic countries following World War II and have not fallen since.

Lutheranism, brought to Australia by refugees seeking a haven from persecution in Germany, remains strong with pockets of followers in South Australia's Barossa Valley and southern New South Wales.

The Greek Orthodox Church is one of the exceptions to the religious decline, continued growth putting it in fourth place among the religious denominations. Its emphasis on a strong family life and pride in ethnic traditions makes it a firm influence within the Greek community. The knowledge among its members that only marriages solemnized within the Church are recognized in Greece makes the bond even tighter.

LEISURE AND PLEASURE

Australians take their leisure seriously. There's a maxim and an Australian tradition that you should "work to live, and not live to work" and pleasure-lovers attempt to live up to this.

The convenience of the family car and increasing leisure time provided by holiday allowances give families the mobility to move further to enjoy the good climate. The nation to all intents and purposes pulls down the shutters and shuts up shop for three or four weeks over the Christmas and New Year period when most of the work force takes its annual holiday.

Even during long holiday weekends such as Easter people are on the move,

OPPOSITE A shipshape boat shed and its peaceful inlet near Sydney, The inlets and waterways make the coastline of the city stretch for hundreds of miles.

long lines of traffic heading out of the cities for a brief break in the country or at some nearby coastal resort.

SUN-BRONZED AUSSIES

Australia is an outdoor society. Come a sunny day - and there are plenty of them throughout the country - the populace looks for some fresh-air pursuit.

With such a large proportion of the population living in cities near the coast, the traditional destination is, not surprisingly, "The Beach". Most Australians can be at the beach within two hours, and because in summer it can become stiflingly hot even a few kilometers inland, it is almost second nature to head for the water to cool off.

Sydney's Bondi Beach has a worldwide image as the typical Aussie beach with crowded brown bodies basking on golden sand while others splash in the shallows, and it is a scene reproduced a hundred times over around the coast on a summer day.

Swimmers cram into a small area of the breakers under the alert eye of a lifesaver who sits high on his elevated chair watching that no swimmer gets into trouble or is swept out to sea by a tidal surge. Just beyond the surf a surfboat is likely to be patrolling the water for sharks, ready to give a warning to clear the water of swimmers if there is any suspicious sighting.

Surf-lifesaving such as this evolved on Sydney's beaches early this century and Australian methods are now emulated throughout the world. No well-used beach is without its volunteer-manned surf-lifesaving club, its members distinctive in their small cotton caps of red and yellow. Each club holds its own annual carnival, and rivalry is keen between clubs. Star performers become local heroes, with the most prestigious laurels going to the winner of the "iron man" race, a stamina-sapping event which involves swim-

33

ming, paddling a malibu surfboard by hand and paddling a surf-ski.

Australia boasts a long history as a top swimming nation, and the standard at carivals is exceptionally high. It is not unusual to find Australia's Olympic representatives competing in club races. The big carnivals attract thousands of spectators and are televised "live"; and floodlit carnivals are another recent innovation.

Lifesaving and the beach scene produced the picture of the tall upstanding sun-bronzed Aussie, at its peak of popularity in the post-war years when the clean-cut image was in vogue and Australia's swimmers and sportsmen were regularly seen on the international winners' rostrum.

SURF SOCIETY

As well as surf-lifesaving, the beach has its surfie sub-culture inhabited by blond-haired youngsters in colorful shorts or diving-suits who can be seen tramping down to the beach at dawn or after school if "the surf is up."

Theirs is a serious dedicated society, whose members regularly spend many hours a few hundred meters offshore, ever-vigilant for the next good wave. Surfies think nothing of driving hun-

ABOVE A night match at Melbourne Cricket Ground. OPPOSITE Hang-gliding and hire boats near Sydney.

dreds of kilometers along the coast to try out a new beach.

With the help of sponsors, the sport has built up a growing professional circuit and the best surfers can now make a living touring the international venues, concentrated in Australia, Hawaii, the west coast of the United States and South Africa.

COUNTRY ADVENTURES

Meanwhile, those who wish to shun the crowd and clamor of the beach head for peace and quiet inland.

The many national parks – New South Wales alone has more than 60 – are endowed with walking trails and tranquil camping sites where you can pitch a tent and enjoy nature for a few days. A surge of interest in rock climbing, abseiling (to descend a steep or vertical rock-face using a rope attached from above and secured to the body) and canyoning in recent years has resulted in some holiday companies concentrating on these sports exclusively.

Other outdoor enthusiasts spend their time canoeing, camping, feasting on fresh fish and swimming in quiet pools. A newer sport is white-water rafting, using an inflatable raft to ride the turbulent waters of the fast-running rivers.

Backpackers and walkers on day-long hikes can choose from the high country, the unpopulated and scenic stretches of coastline or areas rich in historical interest. There is a huge range of treks to choose from. More than a million tourists visit the Mount Kosciusko National Park during summer to walk the ranges and enjoy the wildflowers and views. (This is more than the number of skiers who visit the park's resorts during winter.)

A SPORTSMAN'S PARADISE

Scratch a male Australian and you'll find a sportsman or a sports fan, an en-

thusiast who will support his club or his country with equal fervor.

National sporting fever is at its height in summer during the cricket season, the only true national game when the country is as one. Feelings run particularly high if the traditional arch-enemy, England, is the visiting side, when the two teams compete for the Ashes, that supreme trophy of international cricket. Australia has still not forgiven England for the infamous "bodyline" series of half a century ago when England's fast bowlers aimed for the Australian batsmen's bodies and left them black and blue. Australian fans want revenge and show particular glee if one of their fast bowlers is giving the Englishmen a hard time.

Up to a few years ago there was no more daunting sound in Australian sport than the beer-fortified spectators on Sydney's Hill baying for English blood. Now the grassy mound of the Hill, so long a part of cricketing lore, has been consumed by a concrete stand.

To the uninitiated, a five-day Test match will seem over-long and tedious, particularly when there is no assurance of a result. But to the true cricket fol-lower a Test can be an occasion of high drama, of poetry, of delicate skills, of sheer courage, of fine shades and nuances, all woven into a fascinating encounter.

A new facet has been added to the game in the last few years with the introduction of the one-day game, when the fans are guaranteed a result. It's crash-bash theater which leaves purists wringing their hands and bemoaning the loss of style and skill to the game, but at the same time it has brought crowds of new followers to the sport.

Come winter, and the cricket fans revert to more local loyalties, because there is no national winter sport as such. The various codes of football are split up into strongholds across the country and each goes its own way.

The most zealous fans are in Melbourne, home of Australian Rules football; a game spawned from Gaelic football and virtually unknown beyond Australia's shores. It is played on a large field and involves non-stop play, big kicks and spectacular leaping catches.

In sports-crazy Melbourne tens of thousands will attend an important fixture, while the grand final to decide the

season's champion team will be played in front of a screaming hysterical crowd of more than 100,000 fans. By the time the final matches are played, the city is in the grip of "footie fever" and can think and talk of nothing else.

Sydney concentrates on rugby league and follows the fortunes of its own heroes. The Sydney league competition is the toughest in the world and provides the majority of players that make up the Australian Kangaroos who are currently the best national side in the code. League attendances do not match the Aussie Rules crowds of Melbourne, although on a good day a total of more than 100,000 fans will turn out to watch the half-dozen matches played around Sydney. The game itself is largely financed through lavish social clubs attached to the football clubs.

Rugby union is not so popular and attracts the smallest crowds of all the varieties of football.

It is claimed that fishing has more followers than any other sport, while the leisurely game of lawn bowls has a firm hold across the country and could possibly claim to be the most popular participator national sport.

The days of the 1950s when Australia ruled the worlds of tennis and swimming are now only a fading golden memory, and the country waits and hopes for the emergence of new world champions.

GAMBLING FEVER

Australians are born gamblers and at no time is this more evident than on the afternoon of the first Tuesday in November, the day reserved for the running of the nation's premier horse race, the Melbourne Cup. More than $30 million is wagered on the race, an average of $2 for every man, woman and child in the country. The nation comes to a stop for the running of the event that carries $1 million in prize money, and even the

national parliament adjourns proceedings for a few minutes so the members can watch the race on television.

Punters can also gamble on harness-racing, greyhounds and football matches, providing the State governments, who control all off-course betting and pocket a slice of the action, an annual windfall worth many millions of dollars.

State governments also raise more money through lotteries (the $100 million Sydney Opera House was financed through a lottery), and in the case of New South Wales by taking a percentage of the money put into the thousands of poker machines to be found in social and sports clubs.

When Tasmania opened the Hobart casino about 10 years ago it brought a new dimension to Australian gambling and at the same time did wonders for that State's tourist industry. Other States have followed suit and Australians are playing the tables with enthusiasm, so much so that in the early days of the Gold Coast crowds queued for more than an hour to get into the casinos there.

Sydney is a late starter in the casino stakes, but intends to make up for the lost time by building the world's largest: a 300-table gamblers' paradise that will have almost twice as many tables as the largest casino in the United States.

FESTIVALS

A festival in Australia can be a professionally-run extravaganza such as Melbourne's Moomba or the month-long Festival of Sydney; celebrations where the organizational work goes on year-round and the budget runs into the hundreds of thousands, if not millions of dollars.

OPPOSITE A close finish at Sydney's Rosehill course.

Or it can be a humble day of fun and games among friends in a remote Outback township; organized by an impromptu committee which has to pass around the hat in the pub or at a women's meeting to raise some working capital.

But whether it be a major city or a tiny hamlet, it's rare indeed that any place marked on the map does not have its own special day of the year.

Big city festivals tend to be the most up-market with a cast of thousands, a program that goes on for pages, and an attempt to offer something for everyone. The Festival of Sydney, for instance, brings in expensive orchestras and performing groups from overseas, but also holds a painting competition for small children in the main park.

However the most illustrious festival is Adelaide's Festival of Arts, which invariably puts together an excellent program of Australian and international performers and has gained an international reputation for its high standard. Its success is almost a matter of national prestige, a reaffirmation of the fact that a young country can have a culture all its own.

Having no centuries-old traditions to call upon, Australia's carnival organizers take any reasonable excuse to hold a few days of festivities; for example an anniversary of someone famous once connected with the town, a landmark in the farming year such as gathering in the harvest or celebrating another wine vintage, or maybe it's simply that the town parks and gardens are in full bloom and a floral festival seems warranted.

Some towns have found themselves with floral festivals almost by accident. For example, the city fathers of Grafton in New South Wales planted jacarandas in the streets more than a century ago. About 80 years later someone noticed the beautiful spectacle they presented in the spring when in full flower, and a Jaca-

randa Festival was born. Today throughout the length and breadth of Australia the town is synonymous with jacarandas.

Every flower has its day it seems, but the largest floral festival of all is at Ballarat in Victoria, where by a freak of weather and biological conditions, begonias grow superbly.

The more modest festival in an everyday country town is organized by a band of volunteers and tends to follow a conventional, well-trodden path, adding its own frills and identity as it will. Arts and crafts exhibitions are al-

ways on the program, usually with concerts, a fun fair and a fun run for joggers. And there has to be a queen, some pretty local girl who will be crowned with serious ceremony at the festival ball.

The highlight is a parade through the streets; no festival worthy of the name is without one. The procession of vehicles is decorated with colored papers and balloons, and some will carry a light-hearted setting appropriate to those riding the truck. The local hospital entry tends to favor mock operating theaters, while the scout troop shows off a make-believe camp site. Interspersed between the colorful trucks are bands and groups of marching girls.

Such events help promote community spirit and raise money for charities, while the better-known rural festivals can also bring national recognition to a country town that otherwise would be almost unknown.

Two other occasions which rate highly on the social calendar, particularly in the bush, are the agricultural show and the annual rodeo.

The agricultural show, a tradition transplanted from Britain, gives farmers the chance to compare their livestock and produce with those of their neighbors. There are also arts, crafts and home-produce competitions on the side. The dream of every farmer and stock owner is to win at the "Royal," Sydney's Royal Easter Show, a 10-day agricultural extravaganza which is the showcase of Australia's farming excellence and attracts more than a million visitors each year.

The rodeos follow the American pattern and have produced several riders who have held their own on the tough U.S. professional circuit.

FESTIVALS AROUND AUSTRALIA

NEW SOUTH WALES
SYDNEY
Festival of Sydney (throughout January). A month comprising hundreds of events launched with a spectacular computer-controlled fireworks display over Sydney Harbour starting on the stroke of the New Year. Open-air opera and jazz in The Domain, a ferry race in the harbor, sailing championships, arts exhibitions, and lots more.

Gathering of the Clans (January 1). Highland Games of sword-dancing, caber-tossing, shot-putting and other activities of the Scottish community. Location: Wentworth Park.

Chinese New Year (January or February). Dragon dances, displays of Chinese culture. Location: Chinatown.

Royal Easter Show. The foremost agricultural show in Australia, ten days exhibiting the best farming livestock in the land, and displays of rural produce. Show jumping and rodeo events, as well as firework displays and a fun fair. Location: Royal Agricultural Society showground.

TAMWORTH
Country Music Festival (Australia Day weekend - late January). Thousands of music fans flock in to hear the leading country music bands and attend the presentation of national awards. It's the nearest Australia comes to Nashville. Location: Tamworth is 440 km (275 miles) north of Sydney.

ULLADULLA
Blessing of the Fleet (Easter). The flag-bedecked fishing boats, manned by crews of largely Italian extraction, are blessed by a priest after a religious procession through the streets to the harbor. Location: Ulladulla, on the south coast.

TUMUT
Festival of the Falling Leaf (April-May). The mountain town's deciduous trees put on a brilliant show of color each autumn. Festival activities include a street parade, plaza night, band recitals, a billycart derby and a canoe relay on the Tumut River. Location: Tumut, an hour's drive west of Canberra.

GULGONG
Henry Lawson Birthday Celebrations

OPPOSITE Dinghy sailors use a Sydney harbor-side park to ready their craft for a race.

(June long weekend). The famous bush poet and writer spent his boyhood in this old gold town. Festivities include a poetry and story competition, a colorful street parade, and a musical evening in a gold-rush-era theater. Location: Gulgong is 286 km (178 miles) northwest of Sydney.

GRENFELL

Henry Lawson Festival (June long weekend). Lawson was born here. On the program is a bush dance, street pa-

rade, arts exhibition and other events. Location: Grenfell is 400 km (250 miles) southwest of Sydney.

MUDGEE

Wine Festival (September-October). Six weeks' genteel appreciation of the grape; with tastings at the wineries, wine appreciation talks, champagne breakfasts, a bush picnic, maypole dancing, kite flying and an arts and crafts exhibition. Location: Mudgee is 256 km (160 miles) northwest of Sydney.

BOWRAL

Tulip Festival (October). More than 60,000 tulips flower every spring in town parks and gardens, along with thousands of other flowers such as daffodils. Lilac, rhododendron and flowering shrubs are also in full bloom. Location: Bowral is just over an hour's drive south of Sydney along the Hume Highway.

VICTORIA
MELBOURNE

Moomba (January to early February). Ten days of music and other cultural activities, foot races and a fireworks display, all culminating in Australia's most-watched street parade. A local personality is chosen each year as King of Moomba.

Dragon Boat Festival (Easter). Teams of paddlers compete on the Yarra in festivities aimed at fostering a greater understanding of Chinese traditions.

BALLARAT

Begonia Festival (March). Australia's largest provincial festival honors the begonia; a spectacular floral carpet made of 100,000 begonias woven into designs is the highlight. The best displays are in the Botanic Gardens. The festival also embraces music, theater, a carnival and crafts. Location: Ballarat is 100 km (62 miles) west of Melbourne.

BEECHWORTH

Golden Horseshoes Festival (Easter). According to legend the shoes were made for a circus horse when it appeared in the gold town. There's a grand parade down the main street, an easter egg hunt for children, and wheelbarrow races. Location: Beechworth is 50 km (32 miles) south of Albury.

ECHUCA

Steam Engine Rally (June). Largest display of its kind in the southern hemisphere of steam engines, vintage tractors and historic cars, along with demonstrations of shearing, camp-cooking and spinning. Highlights are a tractor-pull and teams of Clydesdale horses plowing the land. Location: Echuca is on the Murray River 95 km (60 miles) north of Bendigo.

SWAN HILL
Feast of the Lady of Carmel (July). The river town's Italian Social Club has been celebrating the event for more

QUEENSLAND
BRISBANE
Festival of Arts (August/September). A festival which has grown in stature since the opening of the Cultural Centre, attracting leading performers from Australia and abroad in all spheres of the arts.

Warana (blue skies) Spring Festival (late September/early October). A three-week carnival with a street procession, mardi gras, arts and crafts exhibitions

than 20 years, with religious and social activities. The street procession is followed by a carnival and fireworks display.

WYCHEPROOF
King of the Mountain Festival (October). Festivities climax with a footrace up Mt Wycheproof. The climb is only 43 m (140 ft), but each contestant is required to carry a sack of wheat. Location: Wycheproof is 140 km (87 miles) northwest of Bendigo.

held throughout the city, and concerts. Location: Many venues in the city.

CLONCURRY
Merry Muster (August). A festival that concentrates on horses and cattle, with rodeo events and round-ups, as well as a large horse sale and a bush dance.

OPPOSITE AND ABOVE The Festival of Sydney lasts all January. Hundreds of events are on the calendar, many of them informal occasions during which anyone can join in the fun.

Location: Cloncurry is 780 km (300 miles) west of Townsville.

TOWNSVILLE

Pacific Festival (August/September). A lively ten-day festival of street carnivals, a quest for a festival queen and a parade, all celebrating Townsville's tropical ambience. There is also a mardi gras on The Strand every day. Swimmers compete in an 8 km (5 miles) race from Magnetic Island. Arts and culture is also strongly represented. Location: Townsville is 1456 km (905 miles) north of Brisbane.

CLEVELAND

Strawberry Festival (First Saturday in September). The bay-side town is renowned for the juicy strawberries which grow in surrounding fields, and the carnival includes "the world strawberry eating championships." Location: Cleveland is on Moreton Bay on the southeast fringe of Brisbane.

TOOWOOMBA

Carnival of Flowers (September). Queensland's best-known floral festival with a grand street parade of floral floats. Parks and gardens are ablaze with spring flowers of all shades, while private gardens are also open for inspection. Toowoomba is, not surprisingly, known as The Garden City. Location: Toowoomba is 135 km (85 miles) west of Brisbane.

BIRDSVILLE

Picnic Races (September). City folk fly in from all parts of Central Australia or drive hundreds of kilometers, for Australia's best-known bush race meeting. The isolated township's normal population of 80 people is multiplied many times over during the holiday weekend. Location: Birdsville is 1,500 km (930

ABOVE A hot-air balloon at a festival near Sydney. OVERLEAF An ethnic dance group dwarfed by Sydney Opera House.

miles) west of Brisbane.

BOWEN

Gem of the Coral Coast Festival (October). The serious and frivolous both have a place in the festivities. There is a Blessing the Boats ceremony in the fishing fleet harbor and, Bowen being a leading tomato-growing region, a tomato eating competition. Location: Bowen is 150 km (58 miles) south of Townsville.

WARWICK

Rodeo Festival (all October). The month-long festival culminates in the rodeo itself, which attracts roughriders from across Australia and overseas. Among the festival events are a street carnival and art exhibition. Location: Warwick is 160 km (100 miles) southwest of Brisbane.

SOUTH AUSTRALIA
ADELAIDE

Festival of Arts (March, even-numbered years). Australia's best and most prestigious exposition of culture in all fields of the arts, with hundreds of performances and dozens of exhibitions and displays from international and Australian participants. A festival of world ranking. A Fringe Festival run simultaneously offers more unorthodox programs.

HAHNDORF
Schuetzenfest (Second Saturday in January). A German-style festival, centered around a rifle shoot, accompanied by traditional food wine, beer and dancing. Location: Hahndorf is in the Adelaide Hills just outside the city.

RIVERLAND
Harvest Festival (January even-numbered years). Festivities to celebrate the gathering of the citrus, and other crops; with street parades, beauty queen competitions and carnivals and art and craft exhibitions. Location: In Renmark and the other Riverland towns 200 km (125 miles) east of Adelaide.

PENOLA
Grape Zenolian (March of odd-numbered years). A lively celebration of the grape harvest in the Coonawarra wine-growing district, with wine-tastings and a street carnival. Penola is 410 km (255 miles) southeast of Adelaide.

BAROSSA VALLEY
Vintage Festival (begins Easter Monday of odd-numbered years). The nation's premier wine festival, with a distinctly German atmosphere, includes features such as the folk market (Ziegen market) and street carnival (Strassenfes), as well as the family carnival (Gemutlichkeit) at Lyndoch. There are also wine-tastings, the traditional grape-picking championships and grape-treading. Location: In the valley towns, an hour's drive north of Adelaide.

YORKE PENINSULA
Kernewek Lowender-Cornish Happiness-Festival (May holiday weekend, odd-numbered years). A celebration in the "Little Cornwall" region of its Cornish heritage, the tin miners having arrived from England in the nineteenth century. Cornish dancing in the streets in traditional costume, a village green fair in Kadina park, and other events. Location: "Little Cornwall" is 150 km (95 miles) north of Adelaide.

WESTERN AUSTRALIA
PERTH
Festival of Perth (February/March). Three weeks of festivities begin with a traditional opening concert in the Supreme Court gardens. The program includes music, dance, theater, visual arts and outdoor attractions.

BROOME
Shinju Matsuri - Festival of the Pearl (August). A nine-day celebration of this pearling town's colorful past. A Chinese dragon leads off the main street parade, and the program also includes a pearling lugger race, the Ball of the Full Moon and the Sayonara Ball. Ethnic groups put on displays and there are barbecues, fish-bakes and a beach carnival. Broome is 1,190 km (740 miles) southwest of Darwin.

CARNARVON
Tropical Festival (August/September). An exuberant mardigras is the high point of two weeks of celebrations of fishing competitions, a gymkhana, sporting events and a busy cultural program. Carnarvon is 911 km (566 miles) northwest of Perth.

PEMBERTON
King Karri Festival (mid-October). Cultural and sporting events among the big timbers of the karri forest. The town's active groups of artists and craftspeople have a chance to show off their skills. Location: Pemberton is 360 km (225 miles) south of Perth.

YORK
York Fair (October). An historic event

held regularly in the middle of last century then revived in 1971 to finance restoration projects in Western Australia's oldest inland town. There's a traditional flavor about the five days of celebrations. York is 100 km (62 miles) west of Perth.

Wildflowers. Western Australia is renowned for its wildflowers and they are particularly beautiful in the southwest corner. Several thousand species of blossoms, from plants, bushes and trees, bloom between late winter and summer. (See **Western Australia**, page 153.)

TASMANIA
Gum Festival (March). The festival is celebrated State-wide with a large variety of programs drawn from hundreds of cultural and community events.

HOBART
Royal Hobart Regatta (February). The Hobart's aquatic carnival on Derwent River is the largest event of its type in Australia.

EVANDALE
Village Fair (February). Leading talking point of the fair is the national penny-farthing championships, with riders coming from mainland Australia and further overseas to climb aboard their high-wheeled bicycles and race through the village streets. The fair features market and craft stalls, sideshows and street entertainment. Evandale is about 20 km (12 miles) south of Launceston.

NORTHERN TERRITORY
DARWIN
Beer Can Regatta (June). A boat race with a difference, and an indication of the Northern Territory capital's propensity for drinking. Tens of thousands of beer and soft drink cans are used to build a variety of crazy craft, from skiffs and simple rafts to model galleons.

ALICE SPRINGS
Henley-On-Todd Regatta (late August). Australia's strangest regatta—along the dry bed of the Todd River. There are "sea" battles with flour bomb ammunition and "boat" races along metal tracks.

FOOD AND DRINK

There is no such thing as "Australian cuisine." Convicts and early settlers found no indigenous animals worth domesticating and no plants worth eating, so they were forced to breed the livestock and cultivate the vegetables they brought with them. An unimaginative state of affairs revolving around the typical English fare of roast meat and three vegetables followed by a steamed pudding was to persist until recent years. In almost two centuries the only contributions made to a national cuisine have been a meat pie, a dessert and a cake.

The pie is a national institution and can be eaten almost anywhere; on the street, on the run, at the beach or at a football match. News stories appear

from time to time claiming that the pie is not what it used to be, but it is still eaten by the millions every year. Apart from the basic beef pie, it also comes with combinations of onions, vegetables, curry or bacon. It is accompanied by tomato sauce which is smeared liberally over the crust.

Adelaide specializes in a concoction of its own, the Floater; a square pie floating upside-down in a sea of pea soup and crowned with a rich layer of tomato sauce. Stalwarts have been known to eat several in one session.

The uniquely Australian pavlova is a meringue dessert dreamed up by a chef in Perth in honor of the famous dancer, Anna Pavlova. It is filled with fruit such as passion fruit and banana, and topped off with thick whipped cream.

The Lamington, sponge cake covered in chocolate and coconut, and cut into squares, was named after a turn-of-the-century Queensland governor. The apocryphal story of its origins tells of a grazier's wife from the same part of Scotland as the governor, who covered sponge cake in chocolate to prevent it becoming stale. She served it to her husband's shearers as "Lamington's cake".

One British institution which still thrives is the fish and chip shop. A piece of fish is battered and deep-fried until golden brown, then served with french fries; the whole meal being liberally sprinkled with salt and vinegar. Any fish and chips aficionado will tell you that they are at their best when eaten directly from the paper in which they are wrapped. Take-away food bars serve fish and chips along with other fast foods, but for the real thing go to a proper fish and chip shop.

A WORLD OF CUISINES

Australia's Anglo-Saxon palate came to a sharp and timely end after World II with the arrival of European migrants. The change has been so abrupt and recent that even middle-aged Australians can recall going to restaurants when the choice was restricted to either a roast meat or steak.

The Europeans brought with them their traditional dishes, ordinary enough fare to them but a completely new experience to Australians. The modern Aussie can now walk into a restaurant offering any one of a dozen national cuisines and order a meal with confidence.

Every city has a choice of food which reads like a roll call for the United Nations. For example, the cuisine index for Sydney embraces exotic treats such as Balkan, Burmese, Croatian, Czech, Kampuchean, Mauritian, Mongolian, Seychelles and Uruguayan dishes; Chinese and Italian head the list for the largest number of restaurants.

Ethnic restaurants are usually extremely reasonably priced and most follow the splendidly thrifty habit of BYO (Bring Your Own) liquor. Diners are not faced with a wine list priced to take

ABOVE A Dutch touch among the spring blooms at Bowral's Tulip Festival in New South Wales.

in the house mark-up, and can therefore enjoy a more economically priced meal.

At the top end of the price range the variety is just as wide. The capital cities' best restaurants can match menus with any city in the world when it comes to food cooked with flair and imagination.

Part of Australia's new awareness of food is apparent in its appreciation of its local fish, with the result that fish restaurants abound. Sydney's rock oysters rank among the best in the world, while Adelaide has is superlative whiting, Tasmania and Western Australia its crayfish and Queensland its mud crabs.

THE "BARBIE"

The barbecue – or "barbie" as it is known – has become an intrinsic part of Australia's social life in any strata of society. An invitation to a friend's home for Sunday lunch will as likely as not turn out to be a barbecue, while sporting or social clubs wanting to raise money will organize a barbie at some local occasion such as the agricultural show or festival. Barbecue stands can be found in public parks, in national parks, in caravan parks and even in roadside rest areas. In innumerable backyards it is as much a part of the furniture as the clothesline or the wheelbarrow. It can be an old sheet of metal resting on a foundation of bricks, or it can be a fancy heat-maker costing several hundred dollars from a specialty barbecue shop.

Informal barbecues will usually entail nothing more elaborate than throwing some steaks, chops and sausages on to the hot plate, then serving them up with a green salad and bread. During more gracious occasions, the host (a barbecue is one occasion when the man of the house can be boss in the kitchen) will show off his finesse by cooking delicacies such as shrimps or chicken marinated in wine or fish cooked in foil with herbs.

WINE OR BEER?

Wine has only in recent times become a commonly acceptable part of everyday Australian life. Migrants have been largely responsible for the transformation, bringing with them their liking for table wines, and introducing food that calls for a good wine to go with it.

Sales of white wine in particular have shot through the top of the graphs. The two-liter glass flagon and the four-liter cask (a foil bag enclosed in a cardboard

box, complete with tap), has encouraged bulk sales of "vin ordinaire."

Along with increased consumption has come a rise in plantings, and today there are close to 200 wineries throughout Australia. Competition has brought an improvement in overall quality – though the top wines have always been good – and Australia's wines can stand on their own merits. They have qualities of their own, just as distinctive as those produced in Europe and the United States.

However, regardless of the substantial increase in wine-drinking, beer continues to reign supreme as the national drink. Corporate takeovers have absorbed the smaller brewers until the bulk of the market is now consolidated into two giant combines, one of whom produces the Fosters' lager which has become known around the world.

Beers are of the lager variety and are served very cold; in warmer parts of Australia the pubs even keep the glasses in the refrigerator. But be warned – brews are stronger than standard English and American beers. Visitors also find the various measures confusing because they vary from State to State. A half-pint middy in New South Wales becomes a pot in Victoria, while in the warmer climes they serve beer in glasses as small as five ounces.

THE ARTS

The fortunes of Australia's fine arts have waxed and waned over the years, depending on the whim of political fortunes, investors' purses and changing tastes.

At present the performing arts are at the forefront of popularity. Possibly Sydney may have started the upsurge by building the Opera House, a magnificently innovative building which gained world attention for its design and at the same time provided performers with a famous stage. Audiences can attend grand opera, symphony concerts, workshop theater and a variety of exhibitions, all in one exciting building.

Whether spurred on by civic pride or envy other cities have completed new buildings for the arts within the last dozen years.

Melbourne's art gallery houses Australia's most prestigious art collection, while the adjacent three-auditoria theater building contains the nation's largest stage. Adelaide has its riverside Festival Centre, whose halls are designed for flexibility to fit a variety of forms; Brisbane has built a Cultural Centre which brings together a theater, concert hall, the State art gallery, Queensland Museum and the State Library into one complex; Perth's concert hall is for musical presentations from opera to folk, and the 8,000-seat Entertainment Centre is designed for large-scale presentations.

The National Art Gallery in Canberra, completed in the early 1980s, displays a tiny proportion of the 70,000-work National Collection gathered over 60 years.

Record prices are being paid at auction for works by Australian painters of the nineteenth and early twentieth centuries, and the attention which this has attracted has resulted in increased interest in Australian art. Exhibitions of overseas collections regularly draw large crowds.

A number of Australian Broadcasting Corporation-sponsored symphony orchestras are based in State capitals, playing under the batons of world-renowned conductors and featuring soloists of international acclaim.

The standard of opera is extremely high; the Australian Opera, the Victoria State Opera, the Lyric Opera of Queensland and the State Opera of South Australia all produce performances equaling those of any opera companies in the world. As a living symbol of this cultural flowering, Dame Joan Sutherland is idolized wherever she appears.

In the realms of pop music, rock bands such as Men At Work and Air Supply have toured overseas with sell-out concerts; and Olivia Newton-John, the Bee Gees and Peter Allen have topped the pop charts both at home and abroad.

The 1970s saw the resurgence of the Australian movie industry, and films such as *Breaker Morant, Picnic at Hanging Rock* and the *Mad Max* series have won international acclaim and awards.

OPPOSITE Darwin's approach to festival time is larger than life.

49

New South Wales:

The Senior State

SYDNEY: GATEWAY TO AUSTRALIA

If you have just arrived in Australia, the chances are that you will have landed in Sydney - two out of every three visitors do. From an aircraft window the sights of the majestic curve of Sydney Harbour Bridge, the glistening white angles and planes of the Opera House, the harbor itself with its constant bustle of craft of all sizes are straight out of a travel brochure.

ney Cove to set up a penal colony, his original orders had been to found the settlement at Botany Bay, a few kilometers further south. He decided against the Botany Bay site because of its low-lying marshy surrounds (today this shoreline is partly taken up by Sydney airport).

Instead he set out to survey Port Jackson, a large bay a few kilometers to the north, where he found a more suitable site. He raised his flag where the ferry terminal now stands, and the 736 convicts, 211 guards and a handful of

Arrive by sea and you hear the hum of the metropolis as you steam into the harbor between the twin sentinels of North and South Heads. This is a truly cosmopolitan city, abounding in streetwise vitality and young-nation confidence, and yet less than two centuries ago all that existed here was bushland, with the occasional wisp of smoke from an Aboriginal campfire.

INTO THE PAST

When Governor Phillip landed in Syd-

officials set up their tents and crude shelters. However, appalling privations lay ahead and the settlement nearly foundered many times because of starvation, revolts by the convicts and feuding between civil and military authorities. But by far the biggest problem of the developing colony was the failure for almost three decades to find a route over the Blue Mountains, and it was only when the mountain barrier was conquered that the settlement's future was assured.

The Victorian era brought prosperity

to Sydney, and endowed the city with scores of handsome buildings. Many of these remain today, nestling amongst the modern office blocks.

The twentieth century and the two World Wars established Sydney as an industrial city. Most plants are in the west and southwest of the city, regions which have grown since World War II. The population of Sydney has doubled since 1947, and the city is now home to 60 percent of the population of New South Wales.

CRADLE OF THE NATION

So this is where it all began, and Sydney lives proudly and comfortably with its past. A city of contrasts. Next to the Opera House is the cove where the first white men settled, and yet just down the street stands Australia's tallest building, the 304 m (1,000 ft) needle of Centrepoint.

As well as being Australia's oldest and largest city, it is also the most beautifully situated. Sydneysiders are justifiably proud of their city's scenic harbor setting and the 60 km (37 miles) of beaches washed by the waves of the Pacific Ocean.

However, most of the population live rather more than a stone's throw away from the beach. In two centuries Sydney has grown from a settlement of just over 1,000 people to more than three million, with ranks of red-roofed suburbs stretching 55 km (35 miles) inland to the foot of the magnificent Blue Mountains.

Against this natural backdrop of ocean and mountains and with its pleasant semi-tropical climate, Sydney has evolved into an exuberant and gregarious city with an energetic outdoor lifestyle. It is sometimes called brash; Sydneysiders prefer to call it invigorating. At one turn it is slick-smart and poised, yet in the next it can be salty and down-to-earth. It's a place in which both the surfie and the sophisticate get along together. It is above all an easy-going city; the people who live in it know how to enjoy it.

Tourist Information

The New South Wales Government Travel Centre, tel: (02) 231 4444, is at the corner of Pitt and Spring streets near Australia Square and is open weekday office hours. It has a substantial selection of information material.

SEEING SYDNEY

The Old Quarter

Sydney is unique in that it is still possible to stretch out a hand and touch the places where Australia's white history began.

OPPOSITE Sydney's most famous landmarks, the billowing sails of the Opera House and the Harbour Bridge. ABOVE The city's traffic-free plaza, Martin Place, stretches five blocks.

Centre have been transformed into arcades of taverns and craft shops; and old sandstone houses converted into shops selling anything from perfume and opals, to boomerangs and sheepskins.

There is even an authentic village green, surrounded by nineteenth century cottages and the **Garrison Church,** whose walls are adorned with the dusty flags of British regiments of the line who once worshiped here. Sydney's oldest dwelling, **Cadman's Cottage,** stands almost on the shore of Sydney Cove. The Rocks has its own visitors' center at 104 George Street, tel: (02) 274972.

Across the cove, hub of the harbor ferry network, rise the gleaming white sails of Australia's best-known building, the **Opera House.** The Opera House is known around the world for its brilliant and innovative design; a fact which makes Sydneysiders exceedingly proud despite their grumbles about the $100 million it cost them to build. It contains a 1,700-seat main hall, a 1,550-seat auditorium where world-class operas are staged, an intimate theater as well as several other halls. You can walk around the outside at your leisure, but must join a guided tour to see the interior.

Walk out across the Opera House's forecourt and ahead lies perhaps the most delightful street in central Sydney, **Macquarie Street.** The tree-lined avenue is the home of doctors, lawyers, politics and history, and the broad parklands of the Royal Botanic Gardens bordering it along one side give it an extra feeling of spaciousness. Georgian town-houses carrying the brass plates of medical men make this Sydney's equivalent of London's Harley Street. Only two blocks further along is the verandahed colonial building which has housed the State Parliament for 150

The heart of the metropolis clings to Sydney Cove, nowhere more so than **The Rocks** area where the First Fleet arrivals hammered together their first primitive village. Australia's most historic enclave sits in the shadow of the Harbour Bridge and exhibits the heritage of two centuries in its narrow twisting streets connected by flights of steep steps. Hansom cabs mingle with the cars, giving one a picturesque sense of the old and the new.

In the nineteenth century The Rocks was a hell's kitchen and slum, but in the last decade restoration work has begun and what has already been restored displays taste and sensitivity and it has now become a mecca for tourists. Convict-built warehouses such as the **Argyle**

ABOVE Pier One is for casual shopping and entertainment. The Strand Arcade OPPOSITE is more classy.

years. Nearby is the former Royal Mint, now a museum; and across the street be-wigged barristers go about their business at the law courts.

Parks and Gardens

Sydney is exceedingly well supplied with parks, the harbor front **Royal Botanic Gardens** enjoying the prime location. The nation's first public gardens began as a farm planted out with seeds and plants brought by the First Fleet and some trees and shrubs that evolved from those early beds still exist.

Sydney's largest park is **Centennial Park,** whose 220 hectares (550 acres) lie three kilometers (two miles) out of town on the road to Randwick. Horses and cycles can be hired for a ride in the park and this is a popular way to explore the reserve. The road to the park passes Sydney Cricket Ground, scene of many memorable Test matches over the years. Some games are played under flood-lights and make a pleasant night's outing. Behind the ground is Victoria Barracks, whose gate has been manned by sentries continuously for 130 years.

Armies of lunch-time joggers pound along the paths during working days, but at weekends the pace is less strenuous as families enjoy a day out strolling and picnicking in the many gardens.

The adjacent **Domain** is less formal parkland and at its most lively on Sunday afternoons when soapbox orators climb aboard their favorite hobbyhorses at **Speaker's Corner** to sermonize or harangue the audience which inevitably gathers.

A haven of lunch-time relaxation for office workers is **Hyde Park,** 16 hectares (40 acres) of lawns and trees in the heart of the commercial district.

The guard is changed ceremoniously every Tuesday morning, except in high summer.

Touring Sydney

The Sydney Explorer bus tour calls at 20 top attractions, the red buses operating between 9:30 am and 5:30 pm every day. The great thing about the service is that you can stay as long as you wish at one stop, then catch the next Explorer which comes along. Half-day and full-day tours, some incorporating a harbor cruise, are operated by the major coach companies.

The electric train service is a quick

way of getting around the city. Principal rail information offices are at the corner of York and Markets streets, tel: (02) 290 4743, and at Central Station. The York Street office is also the information and booking office for the entire state rail system.

The Urban Transit Authority day and weekly Rover tickets allow unlimited travel on UTA trains, buses and ferries. However if you intend to travel extensively within the State, it pays to invest in a Nurail Pass, which is good for 14 days' unlimited train riding.

bobbing along on a leisurely cruise. Motorboats slide between the sailboats, perhaps heading for the little beaches tucked away in the many bays stretching along the 250 km (160 miles) shoreline. In the quieter stretches, such as Middle Harbour away from the main harbor, much of the shore is uninhabited wooded hillside and the city seems far away.

Seeing the Harbour
The only way to appreciate the harbor fully is from the water. The best-known

The Harbour
Sydney's biggest lure is its magnificent harbor. Governor Phillip described it as "the finest harbour in the world, in which a thousand sails of the line may ride in the most perfect security."

If Sydney Cove is the heart of Sydney, then the harbor is its soul - and its playground. Sydneysiders are energetic water-lovers and appreciate their waterways to the full. The harbor is a lively sight at weekends with hundreds of yachts taking part in races or merely

ride is the half-hour ferry trip to Manly, the traditional resort near North Head, from the Sydney Cove terminal. There is also a hydrofoil service to Manly. Several companies operate cruises from the terminal, and these make very enjoyable outings.

OPPOSITE The convict-built Argyle Centre once a warehouse, now houses shops and taverns; a fountain in Hyde Park. ABOVE Sydneysiders affectionately call the bridge "the coathanger".

SURF AND SAND

Sydney is an outdoor city, and at no time is this more evident than on a sunny summer's day when all roads lead to the beach. It appears that half of Sydney is on the move, cars laden with surfboards and sailboards strapped to the roof, and powerboats or yachts being towed behind. Yet despite the crowds the beaches have room for all.

More than 30 beaches are strung along Sydney's ocean shore, creating one of the world's great natural playgrounds. The majority - and most scenic - are on the **North Shore**, in a 25 km

(15 mile) stretch from **Manly** to **Palm Beach** at the mouth of the Hawkesbury River.

When a surf is running the water is packed with board-riding surfies looking to "crack a big one." These beaches saw the birth of surf-lifesaving, and during any summer weekend a carnival celebrating this will be held on at least one beach. The most exciting event is the boat race, the five-men craft surging on to the beach on the crest of huge breaking wave.

Topless bathing is common, and there are two official nude beaches at **Lady Bay** in the harbor and **Reef Beach** near Manly.

"Bondi" has a truly Australian ring about it, and its beach is synonymous

round the world with Australian beaches and surfing. It is just one of several top beaches on the southern side of the city - others include **Bronte** and **Coogee**.

How to Get There

Buses from the city travel up the northern beaches, but it's much more enjoyable to catch a ferry to Manly and then hop on a government bus going north. The southern beaches are all served by bus routes, and a train runs to Cronulla.

A Word of Warning: Because of the danger of unexpected tidal rips and the occasional shark alarm, each beach is flagged with a swimming area pro-

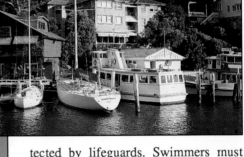

tected by lifeguards. Swimmers must stay within this area. Many beaches have protected enclosures for swimmers.

SHOPPING

Early settlers laid out their paths as convenience and bullock carts dictated, which is why the business district leading back from Sydney Cove is a haphazard pattern of crowded-in streets made to appear even narrower by the tall office blocks.

Streets to the south are more orderly,

The beaches and waterways are Sydney's summer playground. TOP The best-known beach of them all, Bondi.

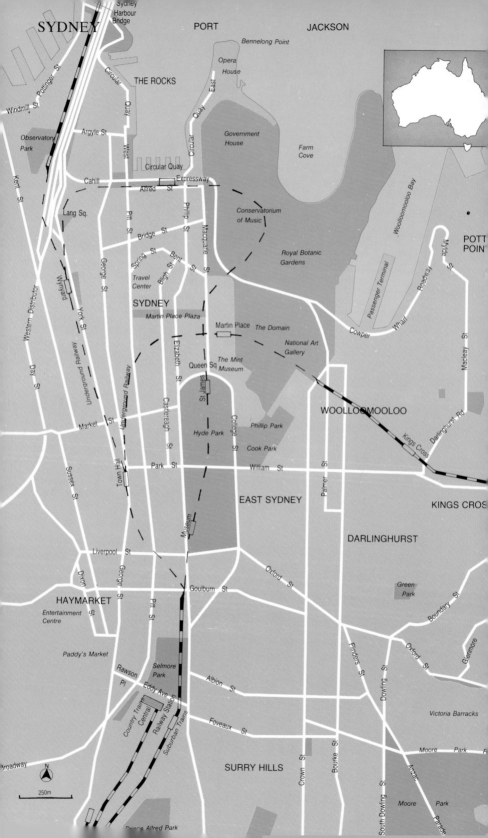

with **Pitt, George** and **Castlereagh** streets forming the heart of the shopping district. Multi-story centers offer a host of shops, while major department stores such as Myers, David Jones and Grace Bros, straddle several blocks joined by elevated walkways. Most shop assistants are familiar with duty-free regulations for overseas visitors. Opals, woolens and sheepskin products are popular purchases, but it pays to shop around for the best price.

Four floors at the base of **Centrepoint Tower** contain over 200 retail businesses. The tower itself is open daily and features two observation decks with access on the podium level. Also on Castlereagh Street is the **MLC Centre**, whose office tower is the tallest in Sydney. Each of the shopping floors, built around a glass-domed hall, has its own theme; from gift shops on the lower level to elegant clothing shops on the higher floors. The complex also houses the **Theatre Royal**, one of the city's major theaters, and several delightful open-air cafes. The 50-story tower in **Australia Square**, one of the city's oldest high-rise landmarks, features a sky-walk observation deck which offers breathtaking views over city and harbor.

A world away in ambience from the modern shopping centers is the nineteenth century **Strand Arcade** in George Street. Its galleries are decorated with wrought iron and polished wooden balconies, while its shop signs are restricted to discreet shingles. In a similar historical vein, art galleries and designer boutiques abound in the trendy suburb of **Paddington**.

All stations on the subway loop except Circular Quay provide easy access to the shopping district.

Just beyond the southern end of the main shopping area in the Haymarket district lies **Chinatown**, with its host of Chinese restaurants, Oriental food shops and even Chinese movie theaters. **Dixon**

Street, the heart of Chinatown, is entered through traditional Oriental gateways which were dedicated only after a soothsayer had chosen the most auspicious day.

More than 1,000 stall-holders cram nearby **Paddy's Market** at weekends and turn it into a noisy cramped bazaar which sells bargains both mundane and bizarre.

Across the street is **Sydney Entertainment Centre**, which plays host to concerts, international tennis tournaments, and trade exhibitions, and other events.

SYDNEY BY NIGHT

The city has always boasted in its own impudent way that it outstrips - in more ways than one - any other Australian city when it comes to nightlife, and few argue with the claim.

Every musical taste is catered for; theater varies from Shakespeare to the latest musical; strip clubs excite those so inclined; nightclubs headline top international acts. If you want to go out for dinner, Sydney's Yellow Pages list 30 pages of restaurants, but the selection after this section may be easier to digest.

ABOVE The Pacific rolls ashore at Bondi, one of 30-odd beaches strung along the extensive Sydney coastline.

Kings Cross is where it's at; Sydney's colorful answer to London's Soho or New York's Broadway. Sidewalks are thronged with the nightly street parade. Glittering lights and winking signs hide some of the warts visible by day, club doormen talk up the attractions inside, the smells from the hot dog carts and steak houses vie with one another and the ears are assailed by the clamor of disco music and pinball parlors.

The Cross is an attraction for many who are drawn to its strip shows, sex shops, adult book stores and mini-skirted street girls; but it also has a host of good restaurants and lively bistros, bars, coffee houses and shops. The **Stables Theatre** in Nimrod Street puts on innovative shows, while in Rosslyn Street across the road tunnel is **Les Girls**, the long-running all-male revue.

George Street, near the town hall, is movieland and Sydney's other main entertainment center. Two theater complexes can screen more than a dozen movies at one time. Hungry moviegoers can choose from nearby restaurants offering international cuisine.

The **Opera House** is something of a misnomer, because it is so much more. The Australian Opera Company and Australian Ballet perform in the opera theater, a larger concert hall is used for orchestral performances by the Sydney Symphony and visiting orchestras, and there is also a drama theater. The view from the Opera House at night across the harbor is something definitely not to be missed.

Juliana's, in the Hilton in George Street, is the undisputed queen of the nightspots where stars of international repute top the bill at the supper club and disco ragers dance until 3 am. **Jamison Street**, situated, not surprisingly, in Jamison Street, has one of the best light-shows in town, while **Rogues**, in Riley Street, Darlinghurst, is renowned for its French cuisine and its disco dancing.

Sydney has long been a stronghold of jazz and many of the well-established clubs are to be found at the top end of town near The Rocks. **Soup Plus** at 383 George Street, and **The Basement**, 29 Reiby Place, are a couple that dish up supper with the hot music.

Unique to Sydney are the glittering club shows, paid for out of the profits from the many rows of poker machines. New South Wales has more than 1,500 licensed clubs run by sporting organizations, service veterans and other common interest groups; the larger clubs attracting world-renowned stars. Tickets for some of these stage shows cost no more than a few dollars.

Tours by Night
Ansett Pioneer, Australian Pacific, AAT and Clipper Coaches all offer night tours, although all the companies only operate Tuesday to Saturday. The earliest tour leaves at 6 pm and the latest gets back

Preserving the past. LEFT Facelift for houses in The

at 1 am. A typical tour lays on free champagne, dinner, a show, and a tour of The Cross. If you want to make your own arrangements, the Friday edition of the Sydney Morning Herald runs a comprehensive entertainment lift-out.

HOTELS AND MOTELS

Hilton International, 259 Pitt Street, tel: (02) 266 0610. 616 rooms and suites. Rates: expensive.
Holiday Inn Menzies, 14 Carrington Street. Tel: (02) 20232. 441 rooms and suites. Rates: expensive.
The Regent, 199 George Street. Tel: (02) 238 0000. 620 rooms and suits. Rates: expensive.
Royal Exhibition Hotel, 86 Chalmers Street, Surrey Hills. Tel: (02) 698 2607. 16 rooms. Rates: average.
Koala Motor Inn Park Regis, corner Castlereagh and Parks streets. Tel: (02) 267 6511. 90 rooms. Rates: average.
Clairmont Village Inn Motel, 5 Ward Avenue, Kings Cross. Tel: (02) 358 2044. 72 units. Rates: average.

New Crest Hotel, 111 Darlinghurst Road, Kings Cross. Tel: (02) 358 2755. 234 rooms and suites. Rates: average.
Hampton Court Hotel, 9 Bayswater Road, Kings Cross. Tel: (02) 357 2711. 126 rooms. Rates: average.
Oxford Towers Motel, 194 Goulburn Street. Tel: (02) 267 8066. 130 units. Rates: average.
Bernly Private Hotel, 15 Springfield Avenue, Kings Cross. Tel: (02) 83 rooms. Rates: budget.
Springfield Lodge Private Hotel, 9 Springfield Avenue, Kings Cross. Tel: (02) 358 3222. 72 rooms. Rates: budget.
Canberra Oriental Private Hotel, 223 Victoria Street, Kings Cross. Tel: (02) 358 3155. 206 rooms. Rates: budget.

RESTAURANTS

Bangkok, 234 Crown Street, East Sydney. Popular with Thai residents, the best recommendation there is.
Butlers, 123 Victoria Street, Potts Point. Stylish French menu, and a view of the city skyline.

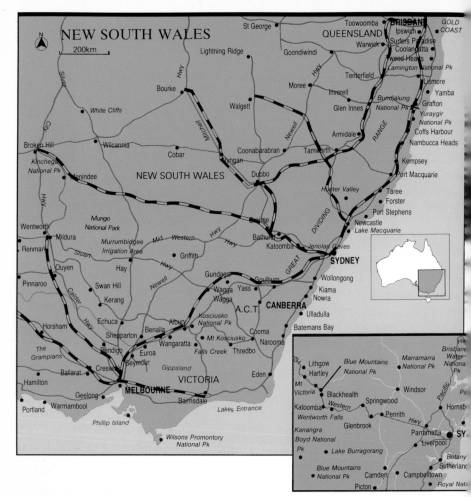

Chinatown Garden, 255 Dixon Street. Mostly Cantonese menu, with excellent dim sum.

Darcy's, 92 Hargrave Street, Paddington. Italian restaurant serving excellent seafood dishes.

Doyles On The Beach, Watson Bay. A fine fish menu and a view up the harbor from the outdoor tables.

Five Doors, 233 Riley Street, Darlinghurst. Classic a la carte menu.

Garden Court, Sheraton-Wentworth Hotel, Phillip Street. Stylish and efficient with an attractive menu.

La Goulue, 17 Alexander Street, Crows Nest. An intriguing French menu that always has some items out of the ordinary.

Lucio's, 47 Windsor Street, Paddington. Try the antipasto.

Turtle's, 225 Oxford Street, Darlinghurst. A French menu with a Swiss influence.

Zia Pina, 90 Mount Street, North Sydney. Hearty traditional Italian food.

HOW TO GET THERE

As well as being the major international gateway into Australia, Sydney is also the hub of the transport network along the eastern seaboard.

By air it's just over an hour from Melbourne or Brisbane, and two hours from Adelaide. By bus, it's a 17-hour ride from Brisbane, 13 hours from Mel-

bourne, 23 hours from Adelaide and two and a half days from Perth, on the other side of the continent. The train journey takes 13 hours from Melbourne, 15 hours from Brisbane and 24 hours from Adelaide. Sydney is also the eastern terminus for the transcontinental Indian Pacific, one of the world's great train journeys, which takes 64 hours from Perth.

OUT OF SYDNEY

THE BLUE MOUNTAINS

The mountains are visible from Sydney, a low smudge on the skyline about an hour by train to the west. And they really do look blue, deriving their name from the haze of eucalyptus oil evaporating in the atmosphere.

Man's encroachment on the sandstone ramparts is confined to the procession of small towns and villages straddling the Great Western Highway, one of only two routes across the range. The mountains, which despite their name are really a 1,000 m (3,280 ft) plateau, form a scenic wilderness of deep valleys and tall eroded cliffs. Most

of the area is a national park and lookouts are clearly signposted.

The main town of **Katoomba** is spread over several hills before coming to an abrupt halt on the brink of cliffs which tumble into the **Jamison Valley**. What is claimed to be the world's steepest railway plunges 250 m (820 ft) down the cliff wall on a 400 m (1,300 ft) track. A cablecar swings out over the valley to give a truly heart-stopping ride.

The limestone caverns at **Jenolan** are about an hour by road further west, with the approach road leaving the highway at Hartley. The caves are open daily.

BATHURST

Another hour's drive along the highway beyond the turn-off to the caverns brings you to **Bathurst**, Australia's oldest inland city. The vigorous farming and manufacturing city has several grand buildings, none more splendid than the century-old Renaissance court house.

ABOVE A quiet street of terraced houses in Kings Cross, a district better known for its racy nightlife.

Bathurst is just a little too far from Sydney for a day trip but it makes a convenient base for visits to Orange, the city 60 km (37 miles) westward which despite its name grows more than half the New South Wales apple crop; and **Carcoar,** another historic village whose bank was the scene of Australia's first bank hold-up.

HOW TO GET THERE

Katoomba is about two hours by train from Sydney, and Bathurst another one and a half hours down the line. The Central West XPT (Express Passenger Train) runs to Bathurst.

Tourist Information
Katoomba information office, tel: (047) 821833, is at Echo Point.

THE HUNTER: VALLEY OF VINEYARDS

Grape vines were among the cargo of the First Fleet two centuries ago, and New South Wales has been making wine virtually ever since.

The 30 vineyards spread over the broad floor and bordering hillsides of the **Hunter Valley,** 160 km (100 miles) north of Sydney, have established an enviable reputation for vintage wines – particularly the reds. The valley is the State's premier wine-producing district, and many of the vineyards have been passed down from generation to generation. The wineries are open during weekdays to casual visitors, and some are also open at weekends if you feel the need for a little more extensive sampling.

The Hunter River reaches the ocean at **Newcastle,** a heavy industrial city of 250,000 people dominated by its steel works and engineering plants and two towering coal loaders. For the second largest city in New South Wales, Newcastle has an undistinguished main street and city center. Its saving graces are a

pleasant park and eight beaches within easy reach. The best view of the city is from Fort Scratchley, a century-old river-mouth fortification.

To the north and south of Newcastle are large bodies of water which in summer become holiday playgrounds. **Port Stephens** to the north is fringed with sandy beaches and resorts, while **Lake Macquarie** to the south has a 160 km (100 mile) shoreline which makes it the largest seaboard lake along the east coast. It is particularly popular with sailors because of its protected waters.

Cruise boats operate on both waters, for those wanting to take a closer look at the area's natural beauty.

If you go to the Hunter Valley or Newcastle along the Pacific Highway, you can step back into history by making a detour near Gosford to **Old Sydney Town,** a recreation of the early settlement. It comes complete with harbor, two sailing vessels, barracks, convict

LEFT Unmistakable shells of the Sydney Opera House. ABOVE Harbor Ferry. OVERLEAF Mellow corner in Hunter Valley winery.

quarters, hawkers and peddlers. There is even street theater and daily "floggings."

Town, while coaches also go there. Tours out of Newcastle go to Port Stephens.

HOW TO GET THERE

Rail services are not convenient for a day-trip to the Hunter, and the best alternative is the three-hour drive by road.

Touring the Hunter

Coach companies operate day tours from Sydney. The State Rail Authority has train-coach trips to Old Sydney

HOTELS AND MOTELS

Pokolbin Wine Village Inn, Broke Road, Pokolbin. Tel: (049) 987600. 54 units and suites. Rates: average.
Newcastle Parkroyal Motel, corner King and Street streets. Tel: (049)

Tranquil scenes on the Hawkesbury River, less than an hour's drive north from downtown Sydney

263777. 138 units. Rates: average.
Civic Casbah Hotel, 465 Hunter Street,
Newcastle. Tel: (049) 22904. 17 rooms.
Rates: budget.

RESTAURANTS

Pokolbin Cellar, Hungerford Hill Wine
Village, Pokolbin. Excellent French
cuisine.
Casuarina, Hermitage Road, Pokolbin.
Flambés are a specialty.

TO THE NORTH

The New South Wales coast becomes
increasingly lush and eventually almost
tropical as it runs north for another 740
km (460 miles) to the Queensland border.

Broad cultivated valleys mark a succession of wide sluggish rivers which
flow toward stretches of coast with such
evocative names as Big River Country
and Summerland. There is even a
"banana republic." Farming and timber
bring prosperity to the towns which dot
the valleys, while small fishing villages
cluster at the river mouths. Dozens of
seaside resorts are crowded in summer
with holiday makers, largely made up of
family groups bent on enjoying the excellent beaches and relaxing in the casual
atmosphere. There is good fishing all
along the coast and in the rivers, while
many families bring canoes, sailboards
and other small craft with them. Caravan
parks, camping grounds and holiday
apartments are usually full during the
Christmas-January school holidays.

Parts of the coast are protected by
some of New South Wales' 60 national
parks, which cover hundreds of square
kilometers of scenic seashore. **Yuraygir
National Park** stretches 60 km (37
miles) along the shore north of Coffs
Harbour, and features secluded beach
retreats separated by rocky headlands.
Visitors come to camp in the bush, canoe,
surf and fish. **Bundjalung National**

Park which stretches along the coast for
another 40 km (25 miles) immediately
to the north has many delightful nature
walks.

Further north is **Port Macquarie,**
which began life as a convict settlement
in 1821 and remained relatively un-
noticed until the 1970s when a population invasion transformed it into a
holiday town and retirement area. This
most historically significant town between Newcastle and the Queensland
border boasts several buildings from the
1820s which have been preserved between the tourist attractions and condominiums.

Another 150 km (95 miles) northward
is Australia's self- proclaimed "banana
republic," the port-cum-resort of **Coffs
Harbour,** hub of the nation's biggest
banana-growing region. This is one of
the few places where the Great Dividing
Range drops almost into the ocean, and
the town is ringed by banana-clad hills.

The town blatantly cashes in on its
banana image, nowhere more obviously than at the Big Banana tourist complex which is hard to miss because of its
10 m (32 ft) fibreglass banana. The
scenery becomes tropical at **Coffs Harbour,** with the banana plantations further north giving way to fields of sugar
cane and the first stilted houses.

Grafton, 80 km (50 miles) further
along the highway, is synonymous with
jacaranda trees and late every October
the streets are a haze of delicate blue from
the flowers of hundreds of trees.

The highway passes through the
growing resort of **Ballina,** site of a gold
rush in the 1860s after gold was found
in the sand. **Tweed Heads** marks the border with Queensland, and Brisbane is
another 140 km (90 miles) along the
highway.

HOW TO GET THERE

Coach companies operate daily services
between Sydney and Brisbane. The Mid

North Coast XPT from Sydney terminates at Kempsey, near Port Macquarie, while other rail services, including an overnight MotoRail, operate to Murwillumbah near the Queensland border.

If you are driving along the coast, make a detour off the highway into the river-gouged slopes of **The Divide,** where rainbow-etched waterfalls plunge toward the ocean, and leafy towns have survived, their tranquillity undisturbed over the years.

SOUTHWARD BOUND

Beyond the heavy industrial city of Wollongong the coast south of Sydney takes on many of the characteristics of the north coast – rich pasture land dotted with dairy herds, placid country towns

ABOVE Sandstone walls of the Blue Mountains National Park. RIGHT These cliffs are perfect for abseilers. OVERLEAF Outsize promotion in the banana-growing region.

and fishing ports and long stretches of empty beaches broken by jutting headlands.

Kiama is a fishing port 40 km (25 miles) south of Wollongong famous for its blowhole, which can reach 60 m (200 ft) when a southeasterly wind blows. **The Terrace,** a row of old cottages, has been restored to house art galleries, craft shops and restaurants.

The rail line terminates 40 km (25 miles) to the south at **Nowra,** the main agricultural and business center of the coast. The high escarpment and plateau immediately inland is **Morton National Park,** a 1,500 sq km (580 sq mile) wilderness of gorges, waterfalls and rainforest, and the home of abundant wildlife including colorful parrots and lyrebirds. The road from Nowra to Neeriga passes through the park, so keep your eyes peeled for the many examples of Australian flora and fauna.

The fishing fleet at **Ulladulla,** another 70 km (44 miles) along the Princes Highway is blessed with religious reverence every Easter.

Just past Narooma is **Central Tilba,** a quaint mountainside village where time seems to have stood still. In 80 years none of its two dozen wooden buildings has been pulled down – and no others have been erected.

Until recent years visitors to **Eden,** 70 km (44 miles) north of the Victorian border and main port of the southern coast, have been able to watch huge hauls of tuna being winched ashore from the fishing fleet. Sadly, catches have declined recently and there are now strong fears for this once prosperous industry.

HOW TO GET THERE

Pioneer Motor Services of Nowra operate bus services which connect with Sydney trains and follow a route along the 325 km (200 mile) coast road to Eden. Air New South Wales aircraft fly into Eden from Sydney.

Touring the Coast

The Princes Highway follows the coast and provides the only road artery. If you don't have a car, you can "bus-hop" from town to town.

Tourist Information

Offices are at Nowra, tel: (044) 210778, and Moruya, tel: (044) 741000.

THE WAY TO MELBOURNE

The road from Sydney to Melbourne takes the **Hume Highway** through 590 km (370 miles) of rolling pastoral land and some of Australia's best sheep country before crossing the State border of the Murray River at Albury.

An hour's drive out of Sydney, the highway passes through the preserved Georgian picture-postcard village of **Berrima,** the only one of its period in New South Wales. The village is known for its art galleries, craft shops and tea shops, as well as **The Surveyor-General,** the oldest pub in New South Wales.

Goulburn, another 90 km (55 miles) to the south and Australia's second oldest inland city, has retained several of its historic homes. **Riversdale,** an old inn built by a convict who made good, is open to the public.

Yass was once considered as the site for the Federal capital, but it was not to be. Iron hitching posts stand on the main street, while on the outskirts is the house of Hamilton Hume, one of the two explorers who pioneered the Sydney-Melbourne route in the 1820s.

Another 105 km (65 miles) up the road lies the town of Gundagai, which perhaps because of its typically Australian name is famed in many a song and poem. Just north of the town stands one of Australia's best-known statues, the Dog on the Tuckerbox. It is part of Australian folklore and a tribute both to the bullock drivers who camped here near the Murrumbidgee River and to the dogs who fiercely guarded their masters' belongings.

HOW TO GET THERE

Coach companies ply the highway, and there is a good train service, including the Riverina XPT from Sydney.

THE OUTBACK

The backbone of the Divide flattens out westward beyond the mountains and

gives visitors to Sydney who may not have the time to explore far into the huge inland a taste of what the interior of Australia is all about – vast landscapes and wide blue skies.

The land stretches over the horizon for more than 1,200 km (800 miles) to the South Australian border, and beyond into the heart of the vast landmass.

The only highway across the center of the State heads out through the rich sheep and wheat country around **Dubbo,** a small go-ahead city worth a stop to visit Australia's only open range zoo

73

and tour the old jail, which is now a museum and still has the scaffold standing in the courtyard. Sale day at the 35 hectare (86 acre) sprawling stockyard on the edge of the city provides visitors with a fascinating look at Australian rural life.

The highway passes through the cotton fields around Trangie and Nyngan, where irrigation has transformed the plains into an area producing three-quarters of Australia's cotton crop.

As you follow the Barrier Highway westward across the plains, it is worth making a detour northward at the Darling River crossing township of Wilcannia, 380 km (236 miles) west of Nyngan. The track leads to **White Cliff,** Australia's oldest opal field, whose surroundings are a moonscape of 50,000 abandoned craters, the litter of 90 years of mining.

Most of the few hundred inhabitants live underground to beat the summer heat. Some of the homes can be visited, so invite yourself in for a peek at a fascinating lifestyle. Two hours' driving westward from Wilcannia lies the largest center of population in the Far West, **Broken Hill,** otherwise known as the legendary Silver City.

A boundary rider stumbled across the fabulously rich ore outcrop by accident a century ago, and the town was born virtually overnight once the news got out. The mines at one time produced one-third of the world's silver.

The School of the Air and the Flying Doctor Service both service the needs of the surrounding Outback families, and visitors can sit in on the classes and be visited by the doctor. On a more down to earth note, a tour of **Delprat's Mine** takes you 120 m (394 ft) underground to appreciate the working conditions of miners. Above ground is a century-old mosque, worshiping place for the Afghan and Indian camel drivers whose trains of beasts supplied outlying stations in the olden days. You can have a look inside on Sunday afternoons.

A distinctive school of Outback art has also grown up in the city and several galleries are open to the public. About 100 km (62 miles) along a sandy track to the northeast among the scrub and rocky outcrops is art of older times, the paintings and imprints of the **Mootwingie** Aboriginal site.

A few kilometers out of town across the saltbush plains lies the ghost town of **Silverton,** remaining much as when history walked away and left it. A century ago it was a booming silver town, then Broken Hill's riches were discovered and the fortune-hunters decamped for the new find.

Wanderer Tours of Broken Hill operate tours to Silverton and Mootwingie.

If you really want to get off the beaten track and have an adventure while in Broken Hill, book a seat on the Bush Mail Run, the light aircraft which every Saturday calls in at 25 remote stations scattered across the vast Outback, delivering mail and other supplies. Traveling only a few thousand feet above the endless plain, you gain a new perspective of the land, forbidding yet with a fascination and harsh beauty. Passengers get morning tea and lunch at a homestead, and are given a first-hand look at the outback way of life and its hospitality.

The Silver City Highway heads south for 260 km (160 miles) to the historic town of Wentworth, but a more interesting alternative route is the road which goes through the quiet riverside hamlet of **Menindee,** and then along the banks of the tree-lined Darling River as it flows south. Explorers Burke and Wills stayed at the Menindee pub during their historic transcontinental journey north in 1860 and you can still see an arrow they carved in a door post.

Just outside the township are the red sand ridges and plains of **Kinchega National Park,** which covers 440 sq km (170 sq miles). The park takes in the sparkling waters of **Lake Menindee** and

also **Lake Cawndilla,** which is an important breeding ground for water birds and the body of water used by Broken Hill's dinghy sailors, who think nothing of the 220 km (137 mile) round-trip drive just to enjoy a sail.

Wanderer Tours offer a day-long trip from Broken Hill to the lakes and national park.

Wentworth is steeped in history. This small town is situated at the most famous river junction in Australia where the Murray River meets the Darling, whose river system is the fourth largest in the world. Last century, Wentworth's prime position made it a bustling inland port and you can still see the paddle steamer *Ruby,* which in bygone days used to ply this part of the river. The hundred year old jail which once housed cattle-thieves is now a museum, and the court house and Anglican church both date back to the 1870s. The town now relies on irrigated farming for a living, and just out of town are orange and avocado groves.

Much of the once drought-ravaged surrounding scrubland has been transformed by irrigation into the district known as the Sunraysia, Australia's largest producer of dried fruits, citrus fruits, vegetables and grapes for wine. The garden city of **Mildura,** across the Murray on the Victorian side, makes two of the longest boasts in Australia – the nation's longest straight street (12 km or 8 miles) and its longest bar (91 m or 300 ft).

A bumpy 100 km (62 mile) ride in a four-wheel drive vehicle along dirt tracks and over the dry saltbush plain northeast of Mildura takes you back 30,000 years.

The oldest known remains of man in Australia have been found in the sun-bleached landscape of **Mungo National Park.** The skeleton of a man estimated to have lived 30,000 years ago has been recovered, along with the buried remains of a woman. These finds on the shore of an ancient lake which dried up 15,000 years ago have forced archeologists to rethink many of their theories concerning Australia's pre-history. A more direct route to Mungo National Park is through

ABOVE Vaucluse House, a Sydney mansion from early colonial times.

Wagga Wagga and along the Sturt Highway. You can also fly from Sydney to Mildura, changing at Griffith, or catch a Sydney-Adelaide express coach and get off at Mildura.

The Sturt Highway runs east from Mildura through the expanding irrigation town of Balranald and across the featureless and seeming endless saltbush flatness of the Hay Plains for 130 km (80 miles) to the town which gave the plains their name. There's an old saying: "The hottest places in New South Wales are Hay, Hell and Booligal

(another town in the region) in that order."

Two hours' drive across the eastern part of the plains leads to the lush greenery of the 2,850 sq km (1,100 sq mile) **Murrumbidgee Irrigation Area (MIA)**; a food bowl growing most of Australia's rice, along with citrus, grapes and vegetables.

Behind the prosperity and tidy orderliness, however, there lurks a darker side. Murders, mysterious disappearances, court cases and drug convictions have in recent years made the name of Griffith, chief town of the MIA, synonymous with drug syndicates and organized crime.

The MIA is a district of the farm-rich Riverina region, whose leading city of Wagga Wagga is the most prosperous and go-ahead in the south of the State. The Murrumbidgee River loops around its outskirts and one of a number of lagoons lies in the middle of town to form the centerpiece of a large park.

HOW TO GET THERE

Several coach tours take in Broken Hill and the southern region of the State, and Air New South Wales flies to Broken Hill. A rail tour to Broken Hill leaves Sydney every Sunday.

Tourist Information

All the main Outback centers have information offices, and the Broken Hill office is located in the old town hall, tel: (080) 6077. The Mildura office, tel: (050) 233619, will tell you how to get to Mungo National Park.

HOTELS AND MOTELS

Old Willyama Motor Inn, 466 Argent Street, Broken Hill. Tel: (080) 883355. 29 suites and units. Rates: average.
Royal Exchange Hotel, corner Argent and Chloride Streets. Tel: (080) 2308. 27 rooms. Rates: budget.
  Grand Hotel, Seventh Avenue, Mildura. Tel: (050) 230511. 119 rooms and suites. Rates: average.
Rosemont Holiday House, 154 Modden Avenue, Mildura. Tel: (050) 231535. 13 rooms. Rates: budget.
Old Wagga Inn Motel, corner Morgan and Tarrcutta Streets, Wagga Wagga. Tel: (069) 216444. 38 units. Rates: average.
William Farrer Hotel, corner Peter and Edward Streets, Wagga Wagga. Tel: (069) 213631. 13 rooms. Rates: budget.

PICTURESQUE NEW ENGLAND

The northeast corner of New South Wales is taken up with the largest highland area in the State. Features of the New England plateau are its basalt peaks, several national parks and a number of State forests.

The university city of **Armidale,** 590 km (367 miles) north of Sydney, is known for its idyllic setting amid inspiring high country scenery complemented by a bracing climate. The city's sedate charm is enhanced by two handsome cathedrals, one of which houses an ecclesiastical museum, a number of private schools set in park-like grounds and playing fields, and some particularly fine late-nineteenth century public buildings. The main street has been transformed into a pedestrian mall and planted with trees and gardens. The city is particularly proud of its parks, which in autumn are ablaze with fiery colors from the deciduous trees planted by early English settlers.

The University of New England was the first seat of learning to be established outside a capital city and stands in spacious surroundings on the outskirts of the city. There is even enough space for a deer reserve. The city's college of advanced education owns the most important art collection outside a capital city, the 1,000-work Howard Hinton collection, which includes works by Arthur Streeton, Tom Roberts, Hans Heysen and other outstanding Australian artists. Hinton conceived the idea of presenting a collection to the college to raise the level of art appreciation through the influence of young teachers. The collection can be seen in the regional art gallery on weekdays and Sunday afteroons.

Glen Innes, a two-hour drive to the north, and **Inverell**, two hours to the northwest, are famed for their sapphires. You can even try your hand at prospecting at Inverell.

HOW TO GET THERE

The Northern Tablelands XPT runs to Armidale. If you are driving, take the New England Highway, or leave the Pacific Highway at either Grafton or near Coffs Harbour and turn inland.

CANBERRA: THE NATIONAL CAPITAL

Canberra is a national capital spawned out of political necessity. It is one of a handful of similar cities around the world, such as Brasilia, Islamabad and Washington, built specifically as the hub of government. In 70 years it has been fashioned into a garden city showpiece by politicians and public servants.

It is this very molding and planned orchestration which its critics claim make it a city without a heart, a city which is not allowed to look inhabited. (Even outdoor television aerials are forbidden.)

The quarter-million residents – and the figure is growing by eight percent a year – live in manicured suburbs of curving tree-lined streets where everything has its place. The swirling patterns of the suburbs' avenues and crescents are a characteristic of the city's plan.

Above all, this is a city of the twentieth century, one with a feeling of space, and one which is tailored to the motor vehicle. Buildings are set well back from the wide roads, swards of parkland and lawn abound, and tall buildings are banned under latter-day restrictions which allow only up to six storys in the town center and three to four storys in other areas.

The focal point is **Lake Burley Griffin,** named in honor of the American architect who in the 1920s won a competition for the design of the capital. The

OPPOSITE The bleached landscape of Mungo National Park, where the earliest evidence of Aboriginal man in Australia has been uncovered.

79

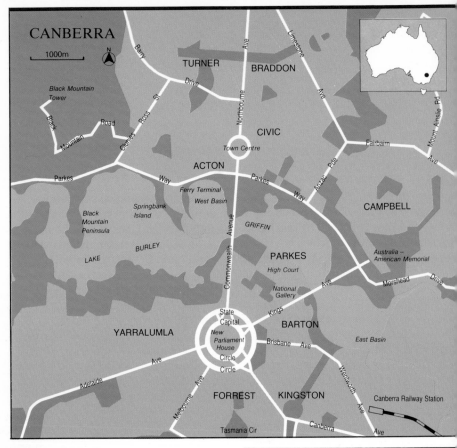

CANBERRA

lake tidily separates the commercial center from the "parliamentary triangle" where the official buildings are situated. Sweeping highways radiate to ever-mushrooming outer suburbs, "new towns" tucked away among the surrounding hills.

Summer is often unbearably hot. In winter, while some days are cool and sunny, cold winds can whip over the nearby Snowy Mountains and make conditions uncomfortable. The wise visitor comes in spring or autumn.

The city stands in the Australian Capital Territory, an area of 2,330 sq km (900 sq miles) specially carved out of New South Wales. Half the Territory is covered with forest, the remainder is pleasantly rolling sheep country rising towards the west to the slopes of the Snowy Mountains.

THE PAST

The valley in which Canberra stands was tranquil pasture for sheep and cattle before fate – and the founding fathers of the Commonwealth – took a hand. Because of the rivalry between Sydney and Melbourne over which was the main city of the continent and therefore deserved to be national capital, it was decided that when the Commonwealth came into being in 1901 neither should be given the distinction. Instead a new city was to be built sufficiently removed from the influences of either city.

The birth of the capital is a succession of stories of disharmony, jealousy between the colonies, and arguments. It took eight years following Federation to choose the site and another quarter of a century to move the parliament from Melbourne.

Two World Wars and a Depression curbed development, and it is only in the last 30 years that the city has grown into its role as the national capital.

On the shores of Lake Burley Griffin stand the **High Court,** the **National Gallery** and the **National Library;** while behind them rises the new **Parliament House,** due to open in 1988 as part of Australia's bicentennial celebrations. It is the completion of this exciting building which the people see as finally setting the seal on the stature of their city.

SEEING THE SIGHTS

The seasons can play an important part in the pleasure of visiting Canberra. Spring is a time of crispness and fresh mornings, while in the autumn the city takes on a mantle of scarlets and golds as its four million imported deciduous trees stage a brilliant show.

As Canberra was built to govern, a tour of Parliament House would seem a good starting point on a tour of the city. A long, low and somewhat unprepossessing building, it had an expected life span of only 50 years when opened. This term will be met when the construction of the new Parliament House rising nearby is completed.

The parliament copies a Westminster system of government, with its accompanying wigs, mace, officials with names such as Black Rod, and diverse legislative procedures. Colonnaded King's Head, the main public area, is lined with portraits of prominent parliamentary figures. Displayed in a glass case is probably the oldest instrument of government brought to Australia, a copy of the Magna Carta which dates from the thirteenth century.

However, the governing of Australia takes place in the **House of Representatives** and the **Senate,** and you can watch proceedings from visitors' galleries. Free half-hour tours take groups through the building and through any

chamber which is not sitting.

A walk toward the lake will bring you to the twin bold lines of the **National Gallery** and the **High Court,** the highest court in the land. The gallery houses the 70,000-work national collection, gathered over 60 years, which includes a large collection of Aboriginal art, as well as the work of white Australian artists ranging from early colonial times to the present day. One of the works to look out for is *Blue Poles,* by American contemporary painter Jackson Pollock, which caused a national furor in the 1970s when it was acquired at a cost of more than a million dollars.

Further along the lake shore stands the **National Library,** which must by law receive a copy of every Australian publication. In its keeping are 1.5 million books and thousands of sound recordings. Changing exhibitions featuring rare and historic documents from the library's collection are on display in the foyer.

Australia reveres its fighting men and pays tribute to them at the **Australian War Memorial,** a shrine to the nation's 102,000 war dead, which is also a museum, art gallery and library. The Memorial each year has 800,000 visitors, far more than any other museum in Australia. It stands at the head of the expansive sweep of **Anzac Parade,** an avenue broad enough to take a military parade of Red Square proportions.

The national **Botanic Gardens** on the lower slopes of Black Mountain, three kilometers (two miles) west of the business district, make up the largest gardens in Australia given over to native flora, the 170,000 plants from all the States and Territories. Visitors can walk through a rain-forest which thrives in a one-time dry gully thanks to hundreds of fine misting sprays controlled by a time-switch. One of several trails leads past trees labeled to explain how they were used by Aborigines.

The mountain is crowned by the 195 m

(640 ft) needle of Black Mountain Tower, a telecommunications link. The tower is open to the public and has the best view of Canberra.

More than 60 countries have diplomatic representation in the city, and many nations have brought interesting new architecture to Canberra by housing their missions in buildings which are like those of their homelands. The Japanese embassy is set in traditional gardens, the Thai embassy is a landmark with its elevated roof and gold-colored tiles, while the Italian embassy blends modern design with the style of ancient Rome. Most chanceries and residences are in Red Hill, Forrest and Yarralumla, and guessing the national flag is a popular game with visitors. The embassies are normally accessible only for official business, but some are open to the public on certain holiday weekends in aid of charity.

The shopping center is to be found close to Civic Square, with a number of complexes containing department stores and a wide range of shops.

OUT OF TOWN

But there is more to the Australian Capital Territory than just Canberra. Rolling hills, rivers in tranquil valleys and both natural and man-made features add to its interest. **Tinbinbilla Space Centre,** on Paddy's River Road southwest of the city, is one of three stations in the world scouring deep space for life on distant planets, as well as tracking manned space vehicles and unmanned craft sent out to Venus, and other planets. At **Tinbinbilla Nature Reserve** it is possible to see Australian wildlife at close range – koalas, kangaroos and other animals are housed in large enclosures into which visitors can enter.

Mt Stromlo Observatory is situated on the same exit road as the space center, but nearer to the city. It houses the Australian National University's de-partment of astronomy and is sited here because of the clear atmosphere surrounding Canberra, making it an important world center for optical astronomy.

The historic mansion of **Lanyon,** near the village of Tharwa, a half-hour drive south of Canberra, is one of a handful of old homes in the Territory. The farm was settled in the 1830s and its out-buildings were constructed by convicts. The main house is a National Trust museum and is well worth a visit.

CANBERRA BY NIGHT

The city is not the most exciting place after dark, and restaurants provide much of the evening interest. The presence of a large international community ensures that it is possible to sample the cuisines of many nations. There are also one or two excellent seafood restaurants to complete the gastronomic choice.

Canberra Theatre Centre in Civic Square is the main venue for the performing arts; its two auditoria stage performances of traveling opera, theater and ballet companies. It is the home of the Canberra Opera and Canberra Philharmonic Society, and a repertory company stages innovative theater at **Theatre 3,** Acton.

HOTELS AND MOTELS

Noahs Lakeside Hotel, London Circuit. Tel: (062) 476244. 223 rooms and suites. Rates: expensive.
Ainslie Hotel, Ainslie Avenue, Braddon. Tel: (062) 485511. 49 rooms. Rates: average.
Captain James Cook Motor Inn, corner Canberra and Sturt Avenues, Griffith. Tel: (062) 953899. 50 units. Rates: average.
Forrest Lodge Motor Inn, 30 National

LEFT Snow gums bent by the alpine winds of Mount Kosciusko National Park. Australia's ski fields are more extensive than those of Switzerland.

Circuit, Forrest. Tel: (062) 953433. 76 units. Rates: average.

RESTAURANTS

Nobb's, Bougainville Street, Manuka. The proprietors term it "modern Australian," which means a menu including venison, chicken, salmon and oysters.
Le Carrousel, Red Hill Lookout. For an excellent meal with an exciting view.
Emperor Court, Yarralumla. Imaginative Chinese dishes that make allowances for diners on salt-free and msg (monosodium glutimate)-free diets.

HOW TO GET THERE

Australian Airlines and Ansett fly in from Sydney and Melbourne as the airport does not handle international traffic. The Canberra Monaro Express train leaves Sydney at 7:30 am daily and arrives at noon, returning at 5:50 pm.

There is no direct route from Melbourne; you must leave the train at Yass and catch a bus. Coach companies operate daily services between the three cities.

Touring Canberra
The city is designed for the car, so renting one makes good sense. A series of drive-yourself tours starts from City Hall in Civic and is clearly signposted. Ansett Pioneer, AAT King's and Murray's provide a range of half-day and full-day coach tours. The companies also operate tours to sheep stations, where a barbecue lunch is laid on.

THE SNOWYS: A WINTER PLAYGROUND

During the winter more than a million skiers and winter sports enthusiasts head for the slopes of the Snowy Mountains,

Australia's biggest snowfield that lies 200 km (125 miles) south of Canberra along the Monaro Highway.

Crowds throng **Thredbo, Perisher Valley, Smiggin Holes** and a few other smaller resorts during the June-September season. Thredbo's setting on the side of a steep slope gives it the air of a European ski village and it is generally acknowledged as the "fast lane" resort; although all have a lively après ski social whirl.

The mountains lie within New South Wales's largest national park, the 6,300 sq km (2,430 sq mile) Kosciusko National Park, and attract visitors year-round. In summer, backpackers tramp the many walks, rope-laden climbers head for rock walls, and fishermen cast their lines into the alpine streams and lakes in the hope of catching trout.

From the top of Thredbo chair lift, which operates year-round, it is an easy eight kilometer (five mile) walk to

Australia's highest point, the 2,210 m (7,249 ft) summit of Mt Kosciusko. The height may be insignificant by world standards, but it is prone to changeable weather and it is essential to carry warm clothing and wear comfortable shoes.

Glacial lakes, limestone caves, windswept moorland and the headwaters of the Murray River all contribute to the park's scenic beauty. The slopes in summer are a carpet of flowers that attract nature lovers and photographers.

The large man-made lakes and dams in the Snowys are part of a complex hydro-electric scheme which took 25 years to build and is Australia's largest single engineering project. Its seven power stations contribute to the electricity supplies of southeast Australia and its waters feed irrigation schemes across three States. The scheme has changed the face of the Snowys, but the associated road system built with it has also opened up the mountains and made them much more accessible.

HOTELS AND MOTELS

Thredbo Alpine Hotel, Thredbo. Tel: (0648) 76333. 66 rooms and suites. Rates: average.
Berntis Mountain Inn Motel, Mowamba Place, Thredbo. Tel: (0648) 76332. 28 units. Rates: average.
Banjos Lodge and Motor Inn Thredbo. Tel: (0648) 76222. 30 units. Rates: average.
The Man From Snowy River Hotel, Mt Kosciusko Road, Perisher Valley. Tel: (0648) 75234. 42 rooms. Rates: average.

RESTAURANTS

Tom Groggin, Thredbo Alpine Hotel, Thredbo. The local mountain trout is a specialty of the house.

HOW TO GET THERE

Coach companies include the mountains on multi-day tour itineraries and also run daytrips from Canberra. Air New South Wales flies into Cooma, about an hour by road from the snow.

OPPOSITE PAGE The Australian Houses of Parliament (background) are set in landscaped parkland on the shores of Lake Burley Griffin. LEFT Campers pitch tent for the night within the sight of the Snowys.

Victoria

The Garden State

MELBOURNE

Australia's second city has a style which is cool and elegant. The home of the Australian Establishment, it considers itself the social capital of the country and arbiter of good taste. Its image is conservative, and it has a reputation for its circumspect and decorous outlook.

Melbournians need no prompting when they proudly remind visitors that for two decades at the beginning of the century (between Federation and the Federal Government eventually moving to Canberra) their city was the seat of national political power; the Commonwealth Government met in the State's Parliament House.

In recent years the skyline has taken on an impersonal profile much like any other in the world, but the city's foundations solidly survive in the distinguished Gothic buildings paid for by the gold from the massive finds of the 1850s.

Melbourne has a flat, uninspiring setting on the Yarra River, but it makes up for any scenic failings in other ways, particularly with its parks, which take up almost a quarter of the inner city area. There are also the beautiful Dandenong Ranges on the eastern fringe of the city and a string of waterfront suburbs and small resorts along the eastern shore of Port Phillip Bay.

The city center itself is laid out in an orderly grid network incorporating wide thoroughfares with room for traffic and space to spare for Australia's only streetcar system. With a sense of fun, one vehicle has been converted into a silver-service restaurant, while another dozen sport the ideas and handiwork of leading artists to brighten the urban scene.

Melbourne is also renowned as being sports-mad. In winter it is gripped by the passions of its own unique brand of Australian Rules football, with the weekly fortunes of the teams being followed obsessively in the media and the

pubs. The nation's premier horse race, the Melbourne Cup, brings the country to a halt every November; and its cricket ground is far and away the biggest in the land, holding a world record 90,000 strong cricket crowd. Up to 120,000 have even crammed in for football matches such as the Australian Rules Grand Final in September.

MELBOURNE'S PAST

The site of Melbourne was "bought" from Aborigines for a few dollars in the form of flour, blankets and other trading goods in 1835 by one John Batman, who was the vanguard of an invasion of land-seekers from Tasmania. A sufficient number of enterprising settlers, determined to shed themselves of Sydney's officialdom and establish a settlement free from the taint of the penal system, found what they wanted in Port Phillip Bay. The defiant pioneers prospered and achieved their separation from Sydney only 16 years after Batman's bargain.

That same year saw the first of the rich Victorian gold strikes, and Melbourne suddenly found itself free and wealthy. The foundling city did not so much grow, it exploded as streams of prospectors poured in from all parts of the world.

From the wealth and attendant prestige rose the richly endowed public and private buildings, the cathedrals and the magnificent mansions of the merchants.

Within a decade of the first rush, Melbourne had surpassed Sydney as Australia's most populated city, and within a few more years it had also become the nation's business capital. Sydney regained the population crown in the first few years of this century, but it was only in the early 1980s that Sydney could again claim with confidence to be

LEFT Century-old army barracks in Melbourne. BELOW Rowing eights limber up in the heart of the city.

the financial and business hub - and even then Melbourne would only grudgingly concede this loss of status.

The post-war wave of migrants has increased the population to 2.7 million and made its mark with shops and restaurants reminiscent of those from European and Asian homelands, all of which makes a visit to Melbourne a truly cosmopolitan experience.

Tourist Information

First stop should be the Victorian Government Travel Centre, at 230 Collins

The most famous thoroughfare, **Collins Street**, differs in mood and pace along its length. At its eastern end, which is still sometimes referred to as the Paris End, plane trees shade the sidewalk tables of coffee shops, which rub shoulders with discreet boutiques and graceful art galleries. Many of the classic baroque buildings of the last century have been replaced by modern towers of commerce, yet sufficient remain to make the street a fascinating mix. Down the hill is the **Uniting Church**, which stands on the site of Melbourne's earli-

Street, between Swanston and Elizabeth streets, tel: (03) 6119944. The center is open weekdays during office hours, and Saturday mornings. The Melbourne Age information center, tel: (03) 675831, is a weekday telephone service.

est permanent church, and Victoria's oldest Baptist church, built only 10 years after Batman stepped ashore.

The noble town hall is now seen to better advantage with the development of the open space of **City Square**, with its sunken amphitheater and its waterfalls. You are now in the heart of the shopping district, with its numerous arcades and department stores. At the corner of Elizabeth Street stands the **CML Building** where from the 21st floor you can get a bird's-eye view of

CITY STROLLS

The grid system of the central shopping and business district makes it easy to find your way around, and the area is surprisingly compact.

he city (weekdays at 2:30 pm). The Stock Exchange, at No. 351, has a gallery from which visitors can watch the trading floor.

From downtown, looking back up Bourke Street towards Spring Street you cannot miss the classic stone bulk of Victoria's **Parliament House**, which is still waiting to be finished despite building work beginning in 1856, - a 45 m (147 ft) dome has still not materialized. Tours of the lavish interior are conducted on weekdays. Around the corner in Albert Street stands Australia's largest place of worship, **St Patrick's Roman Catholic Cathedral**, an outstanding example of Gothic architecture.

PARKS AND GARDENS

When the heart of Melbourne was being laid out 130 years ago, wise city fathers deemed that there should be ample open space. Today there are more than 400 parks, gardens and recreation areas in the metropolis, several of them extending in one great sward around the southeast corner of the business area.

A streetcar going east along Flinders Street will drop you off at **Fitzroy Gardens**, just across the road from the Hilton Hotel. Fitzroy Gardens, along with neighboring **Treasury Gardens**, are Melbourne's oldest and are popular with office workers at lunch-time and with families for weekend strolls. The cottage of the parents of Captain Cook, crated from England and re-erected to mark Melbourne's centenary, looks for all the world as if it had never left its native English garden.

Across Wellington Parade you will find **Yarra Park**, home of the Melbourne Cricket Ground, Australia's largest sports stadium and main setting for the 1956 Olympic Games. A footbridge across the railroad leads to **Olympic Park**, with its various playing fields and swimming pool, and another two bridges across the Yarra brings you into

the large parkland of **Kings Domain** and **Queen Victoria Gardens**, once the site of a shanty town for goldminers. Here stands the **Myer Music Bowl**, venue for many outdoor entertainment events. Up to 20,000 can be seated on the lawns during concerts, and double this number have been known to cram in on special occasions. On the eastern side of the Domain is the **Royal Botanic Gardens**, one of the best examples in the world of landscaping and recognized as the most impressive gardens in Australia.

HOME OF THE ARTS

It is easy to find Melbourne's brilliant new **Arts Centre** - just aim for the 115 m (380 ft) lattice spire across the river from Flinders Street railroad station. The **National Gallery** - it retains its name despite the opening in Canberra of the Australian National Gallery - houses a superb collection of world ranking, as well as an extensive collection of Aboriginal art. Study galleries have been thoughtfully provided for visitors to examine works not on display. The theater complex itself contains three auditoria. The center's information pavilion, tel: (03) 11566, is open daily and will give you details of programs.

LEFT St Paul's Cathedral and Civic Square, and the mogul façade of a theater. ABOVE Art in the park.

In **Russell Street** are the **National Museum of Australia** - with Australia's only **Children's Museum** - and **Old Melbourne Gaol**, where Australia's most famous outlaw, Ned Kelly, was hanged. Not surprisingly, sports-crazy Melbourne has two sporting museums. The **Horseracing Museum**, at the **Caulfield Track**, is open on race days, and the **Cricket Ground Museum** is open to groups on Wednesdays.

THE LIVELY SUBURBS

Melbourne's suburbs stretch 60 km (37 miles) around the shores of Port Phillip Bay and to the Dandenong foothills and are a fascinating mixture of social strata, migrant backgrounds and architectural disciplines.

Carlton, 10 minutes in a streetcar from downtown, is usually referred to as "**Little Italy**;" its migrants brought their restaurants, espresso bars and pavement cafés to the previously quiet streets. **Lygon Street** at night is the liveliest street in town, frequented by students from the nearby university. The next-door suburb of **Fitzroy** has been revived with the influx of restaurants, antique shops and other small businesses. The southern fringe of Fitzroy, **Victoria Street**, takes on an Asian flavor as it heads eastward and passes through **North Richmond**. Melbourne's Vietnamese community can sell you anything from a silk dress to pink and green jelly cakes; all this makes for an interesting afternoon's browsing.

South Yarra, across the river, and neighboring **Toorak**, are considered the smart suburbs. Elegant mansions line the shady streets and well-heeled trend-setters and jet-setters window-shop and browse in fancy food shops and boutiques. One of the grandest houses of all, the historic mansion called **Como House**,

LEFT The gold-rush days live on at Sovereign Hill, a reconstructed mining town at Ballarat.

93

in **South Yarra**, now belongs to the National Trust and is open daily.

When Melbournians want some fun they automatically head for **St Kilda**, the bay-side suburb only a short streetcar ride from the city. A fun-fair offers all the old favorite rides, and there is a skating rink, a **Palais de Danse**, and the **Palais Theatre** - an enormous hall which is a hang-over from the music hall days.

HOW TO GET THERE

All these suburbs are on the metropolitan train network, or on a tram route. A No. 8 tram will take you from Swanston street to Toorak and South Yarra, and a No. 15 to St Kilda.

SHOPS GALORE

The boundaries of the shopping district are formed by **Exhibition, Collins, Elizabeth** and **Londsdale** streets and these dozen blocks house a profusion of products for all tastes. Australia's largest department store, **Myers**, is one of many to be found in **Bourke Street**; while the stores of **Collins Street** and **Little Collins Street** epitomize elegance and international haute couture. **Georges** in Collins Street is Melbourne's most elegant department store, while **Swanston Street** and **Elizabeth Street** are lined with fancy-goods and small specialty shops.

Arcades are a feature of shopping in Melbourne and none are more glamorous than **City Square** on the corner of Collins and Swanston streets. Here you can get anything from a fluffy souvenir to bullion, a sandwich to a haircut. There are numerous indoor and outdoor restaurants, and a tavern whose four bars are a watering hole for homeward bound office workers and a rendezvous before a night on the town.

The oldest arcade, the gracious **Royal Arcade**, fronts on to **Bourke Street**

Mall, a section of the street which has been blocked to all traffic but streetcars, and has become a performing stage for buskers.

A good shopping area away from the main center is South Yarra's **Chapel Street**, with its avant-garde boutiques, bric-a-brac shops and Australian businesses. Call in at the **Jam Factory**, a magnet for those who set the trends in fashion and food. The other main venue to rub shoulders with the beautiful people is **Toorak Road** in neighboring **Toorak** (pronounce it T'rak and the natives will take you for one of their own). Across the rail line is **Armadale**, whose **High Street** is the hub of Melbourne's antique trade.

Melbournians are inveterate bargain-hunters and haunt the old-fashioned markets, which are an institution in themselves. The **Queen Victoria Market**, at the top of Elizabeth Street, sets up shop each day except Monday. You can also have fun rummaging around markets in **Camberwell, Croydon, Dingley, Footscray** and several other suburbs. Ask the travel center for details.

Opal dealers can be found in **Howey**

Place, **Collins Street**, and the **Southern Cross Plaza**. Aboriginal crafts are also available in the plaza, as well as at **50 Bourke Street**. Best place to look over the work of local craftsmen is in the converted meat market at **Courtney Street, North Melbourne**, near the Queen Victoria Market.

TOURING MELBOURNE

The Met ticket allows you to use all modes of the excellent public transport network - train, tram and bus - for the price of one ticket; while a Travel Card will get you around for a day or a week. The Transport Information Centre telephone number is (03) 617 0900. City Explorer buses leave Flinders Street station on the hour from 10 am to 4 pm. The coach companies all operate city sightseeing tours.

If you intend to travel around Victoria, ask the Travel Centre staff for details or contact the State rail system V/Line, tel: (03) 623115, for details of

LEFT Classical lines of Melbourne's Exhibition Building. ABOVE A city center haven in Collins Place.

its Super Savers rail services and Day Away tours.

MELBOURNE BY NIGHT

Despite Melbourne's straitlaced reputation (and in today's liberated times that distinction is apocryphal), she loosens her corsets when the sun goes down.

Diners have a choice of 1,300 restaurants and a whole gamut of worldwide cuisines. **Chinatown** and its restaurants offering dishes from all the culinary regions of China is in **Little Bourke Street**. For other ethnic food try **Swan Street** in **Richmond** for Greek dishes, the Turkish restaurants and cafés in **Sydney Road, Brunswick**, and **Lygon Street, Carlton** if you prefer Italian food. **Spaghetti Graffiti** in Chapel Street, South Yarra, and **Johnny's Green Room**, in Faraday Street, Carlton, are both open 24 hours a day.

The nearest Melbourne comes to London's West End or New York's Broadway is at the eastern end of **Bourke Street**, where neon signs light up the movie theater marquees. Discos, night clubs and other after-dark entertainment is scattered throughout the inner city and suburbs.

The **Underground Discotheque** in King Street has rocked on for several years, **Inflation** is another disco just along the street and **Cabaret Fame** is at the northern end of Swanston Street in Carlton. The sweet young things of Toorak and South Yarra frequent **Broadway, Chasers** and **Silvers**, while homosexuals congregate at **Mandate** in Carlisle Street, St Kilda.

Theater has always been good in Melbourne, and the arts now make a greater impact because so much can be staged under one roof at the **Arts Centre**. The Australian Ballet, Australian Opera, Victorian State Opera, Melbourne Symphony Orchestra and Melbourne Theatre Company all perform here.

It pays to drop in at **Half-Tix**, a booth in Bourke Street mall which sells a range of theater tickets at half-price on the day of the performance.

A lively and constantly-changing music scene lets its hair down in the pubs and clubs. Much of the action is out in the suburbs, and the best way to keep in touch is through the entertainment sections of the newspapers.

Tours By Night

For some obscure reason there is no combined "coach-drinks-meal-tour of the city" package available in Melbourne, so you just have to make your own arrangements. If you want an exclusive tour, the Melbourne Tour Company, tel: (03) 439 6282, brings a chauffeured car to your door and you are driven around the city sights for four hours, stopping off for a cocktail at a club, but no meal.

HOTELS AND MOTELS

Hilton, 192 Wellington Parade, East Melbourne. Tel: (03) 419 3311. 413 rooms and suites. Rates: expensive.

Menzies At Rialto, 495 Collins Street. Tel: (03) 620111. 254 rooms and suites. Rates: expensive.

Southern Cross, 131 Exhibition Street. Tel: (03) 654 0221. 469 rooms and suites. Rates: expensive.

Astoria City Travel Inn, 288 Spencer Street. Tel: (03) 676801. 36 rooms and suites. Rates: average.

Ramada Inn, 539 Royal Parade, Parkville. Tel: (03) 380 8131. 41 units. Rates: average.

Downtowner Motel, 66 Lygon Street, Carlton. Tel: (03) 663 5555. 89 units. Rates: average.

Lygon Lodge, 220 Lygon Street. Tel: (03) 663 6633. 66 units. Rates: average.

Crossley Lodge Motel, 51 Little Bourke Street. Tel: (03) 662 2500. 74 units. Rates: average.

Queen's Bridge Family Hotel, 1 Queensbridge Street, South Melbourne. Tel: (03) 613117, 18 rooms. Rates: budget.

Royal Arcade Hotel, 301 Little Collin Street. Tel: (03) 638695. 21 rooms. Rates: budget.

Kingsgate Private Hotel, 131 King Street. Tel: (03) 624171, 232 rooms. Rates: budget.

Miami Private Hotel, 13 Hawke Street, West Melbourne. Tel: (03) 329 8499. 104 rooms. Rates: budget.

RESTAURANTS

Avanti, 235 Ratdowne Street, Carlton. Home-made pasta complements the other dishes, with fresh fish also a specialty.

Barbarino's, 454 St Kilda Road, Melbourne. A taste from home for any American diners. Barbecued ribs are a specialty.

Basilea, 408 Burke Street, South Camberwell. A Swiss menu, with their Swiss veal one of the most popular items.

Cafe Florentino, 80 Bourke Street. A byword in Melbourne for years for its authentic French and Italian cooking.

Colonial Tramcar. Meals on wheels with a difference. Food good although not fantastic.

Empress of China, 120 Little Bourke Street. Chinese Cantonese cuisine invariably of the highest standard.

Flower Drum, 103 Little Bourke Street. Top Cantonese cuisine.

Glo Glo's, 3 Carters Avenue, Toorak. Superb French dishes with an extensive wine list. A very stylish restaurant.

Jean Jacques, 502 Queensberry Street, North Melbourne. Seafood the French way, with such dishes as Terrine of Eel in Pastry, and an excellent bouillabaisse.

La Cacciatora, 29 Grattan Street, Carlton. Serves some of the best game in town.

RIGHT The last glows of sunset light up the concrete and glass towers of Melbourne's business district.

Lazar's Charcoal Grill, 87 Johnston Street, Fitzroy. No menu, just choose your own steak, and follow it up with strawberry pancakes.

Onions, 50 Commercial Road, Prahran. Good selection of superbly cooked dishes, mainly meat, simply presented.

Phantom India, 427 Swanston Street, Carlton. Specializes in dishes from northern India.

Plaka, 1438 Malvern Road, Malvern. A Greek tavern with an informal atmosphere. Goat kebab is on the menu from time to time.

Rasa Singapura, 648 Glenferrie Road, Hawthorn. Specializes in Nonya cooking, a marriage of Malaysian and Chinese styles of cooking.

Sheik Omar, 194 Commercial Road, Prahran. A set menu of 12 Lebanese dishes, eaten under a tent roof. For those interested in Oriental delights, wait for the belly dancer who performs later in the evening.

Sukiyaki House, 21 Alfred Place, Melbourne. Traditional Japanese restaurant, complete with a sushi bar.

Tu-Do, 143 La Trobe Street, Melbourne. Excellent variety of regional food from Vietnam.

HOW TO GET THERE

Melbourne airport is an international gateway and the city is also well served by interstate airlines, railway and interstate coach services. V/Line operates MotoRail trains between Melbourne and Sydney, Adelaide and Mildura.

OUT OF MELBOURNE

Despite their Aboriginal name of Tanjenong (high mountains), the forested **Dandenong Ranges** are nowhere more than 630 m (2,060 ft) high. The hills are about an hour out of Melbourne on the metropolitan train system and are the most popular day-trip destination for visitors. The small towns and villages which dot the slopes were hacked out of the bush by pioneers who stayed to farm the valley floors, cut wood and grow vines.

The city rail line goes to Lilydale, a long-established township. A bus service runs from here to **Yarra Glen**, a settlement which was an early wine-growing area and now supports half a dozen vineyards, and on to the resort of **Healesville**. Here you can stroll among the emus, ibis, kangaroos and parrots at **Healesville Sanctuary**, and stroke the koalas.

Another rail line branches south to **Ferntree Gully**, where a small national park is a haven for more than 100 species of birds. The park is criss-crossed with many walks for the more energetic. Off the rail line but only 10 km (six miles) by road from Upper Ferntree Gully station is the village of **Olinda**, famous for its **National Rhododendron Gardens** (the blooms are best in October), and the **William Ricketts Sanctuary**, where the story of the Aboriginal people is portrayed in figures sculpted by Ricketts.

The railroad terminates at **Belgrave**, the Dandenongs' shopping and commercial center, but a quaint narrow-gauge steam train takes over at weekends and holidays. Puffing Billy is the only surviving locomotive of its era and it chugs through the gullies and valleys for 13 km (8 miles) to the hill town of **Emerald**, which despite its name grew out of a gold strike.

HOW TO GET THERE

Inquire at the Travel Centre or transport information office for times of trains and connecting buses, or take a coach tour - AAT King's, Ansett Pioneer and Australian Pacific all have services.

LEFT A landmark of the '80s, the 116 m (380 ft) spire of Melbourne's Arts Centre, home of a superb art collection.

Healesville Railway Co-op operates a day trip from Spencer Street station to two Yarra Glen wineries and a wine expert will be on board to answer passengers' questions.

PORT PHILLIP BAY

At its broadest point **Port Phillip Bay** is 65 km (40 miles) and has a shoreline of 225 km (140 miles). Perhaps the best way to appreciate its vast expanse is to take a trip down the boot-shaped **Mornington Peninsula**. Its 90 km (55 mile) long crescent shore is virtually one long beach from the outskirts of Melbourne to its tip, and it is a favorite destination for Melbourne folk on either day trips or annual holidays. The narrowness of the ocean entrance to the bay causes it to have little tide and virtually no current except near the entrance, and is therefore ideal for sailing, swimming and most water sports.

The bay-side resorts have retained much of their rural atmosphere despite the increasing development of the city and on summer days are a magnet for tens of thousands of urban dwellers. Some of the holiday towns even cling to their delightful privately-owned bathing huts, a bit of old-fashioned "one upmanship" in an egalitarian world.

The railroad line only follows the shore halfway down the peninsula to **Frankston**, 40 km (25 miles) out of Melbourne, so the most convenient way to see all the peninsula is on a coach tour. The coast road passes through **Mornington**, which has retained its charm as a fishing port despite the onslaught of city dwellers, and another 17 km (11 miles) later arrives at Dromana, where a chair lift will take you to the top of **Arthur's Seat**, behind the township. The 314 m (1,030 ft) summit is the highest point along the coast, and from this vantage point you can look out over the gently rolling farmlands of the southern part of the peninsula and

across the bay to the Bellarine peninsula 30 km (18 miles) away. **Portsea**, at the end of the peninsula, is the resort where Melbourne's high society spends summer days in its many mansions and weekend cottages.

A motor rail service from Frankston can take you across the peninsula to the smaller, and much quieter, **Western Port Bay**. Stony Point is the departure point for the ferry service to **Phillip Island**. A fascinating place to head for is **Summerland Beach**, on the southern side of the island, where several thousand fairy penguins can be seen every evening waddling up the beach to their burrows in the dunes seemingly oblivious of the hordes of visitors who have come to watch the spectacle.

HOW TO GET THERE

Apart from the train/ferry service to Phillip Island, there are a number of coach tours, some of which also take in the Dandenongs. It is possible to drive on to Phillip Island by following the Bass Highway. Molony Aviation flies a 30-minute Penguin Express to Phillip Island timed for the evening ceremony.

BALLARAT

The fine buildings and extravagant villas of the boom days of this elegant city of Victoria's central goldfields are monuments to the wealth extracted from the diggings.

The State's largest inland city with a population of 60,000, **Ballarat** is only 112 km (70 miles) west of Melbourne and has matured from a rough tent and shantytown of the 1850s into a gracious provincial center. The main street, **Sturt Road**, is a wide thoroughfare flanked by many of the 60 nineteenth century buildings recognized by the National Trust. Just off the street, in Lydiard Street North, the **Fine Art Gallery** houses an important collection of Australian works. Also on display is the flag flown by rebel miners in 1854 at Eureka Stockade in the only civil battle in Australia's history. A replica of the fortifications defended by the miners can be seen in **Eureka Stockade Park**, a couple of blocks south of the Western Highway. Miners were attacked by government troopers for refusing to pay their licensing fees and in the ensuing fight 22 miners and six of

the attackers died.

The 40 hectares (100 acres) botanical gardens are the most outstanding in country Victoria and in March are brilliant with the begonias for which the city is famous.

If you want to step back into the lively gold-rush era, the reconstructed mining township of **Sovereign Hill** is steeped in the flavor of the diggings. The main street represents the old Main Road, Ballarat, as it was 150 years ago. It's a working township, with a smithy, bakery, candy shop and hotel all open for business, and "mining" going on at the diggings. A mine has been turned into a museum that graphically recreates the atmosphere and spirit of the "good old days."

Tourist Information
The Central Highlands Tourist Authority office is at Bakery Hill, tel: (053) 322694.

HOTELS AND MOTELS

Mid City Motel, 19 Doveton Street North. Tel: (053) 311222. 67 rooms.

ABOVE Private bathing huts, quaintly reminiscent of Edwardian times (graffiti apart) at a bayside resort.

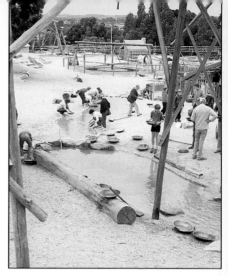

ABOVE Reliving history at Sovereign Hill. BELOW Queen Victoria overlooks Ballarat Town Hall. RIGHT William Ricketts Sanctuary in the Dandenongs.

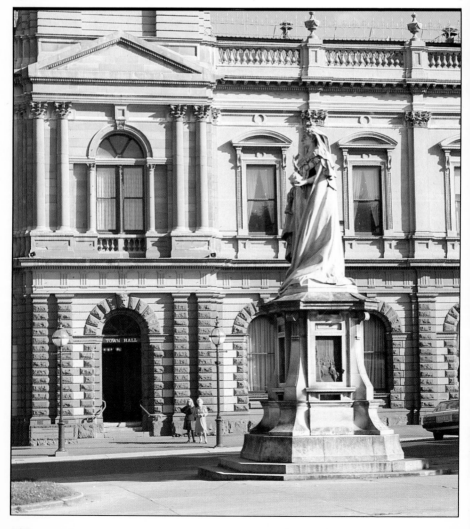

Rates: average.

Craigs Royal Hotel, 10 Lydiard Street South. Tel: (053) 311377. 49 rooms. Rates: average.

Brewery Tap Motel, Western Highway. Tel: (053) 347201. 14 units. Rates: budget.

RESTAURANT

La Scala, 120 Lydiard Street. Regarded by many diners as Victoria's best country restaurant.

HOW TO GET THERE

Ballarat is 1 hour 45 minutes by rail from Melbourne, and V/Line operates Day Away tours daily except Sunday. Coach companies also run day trips from Melbourne.

GOLD RUSH COUNTRY

Victoria's rip-roaring gold rush country of last century is now fertile rolling countryside dotted with small towns reached along the Midland Highway, north of Ballarat. Communities once tens of thousands strong have vanished, others linger on in serene farming towns.

Overgrown waste heaps, dangerous mine shafts and discarded machinery scar the landscape.

CRESWICK

Creswick, 18 km (11 miles) up the highway from Ballarat, was at bursting point in the 1860s, as 60,000 people toiled for gold. It's difficult to believe that now, as you drive through the quiet little township. A 20 km (12 mile) detour along the Maryborough road leads to **Clunes**, where the Victorian bonanza began in 1851 when James "Civil Jim" Edmonds made his historic strike. Victoria's oldest gold town is worth visiting, if only for its sense of history and striking location in a valley surrounded by 22 extinct volcanoes.

Sufferers from aches and pains have great faith in the curative qualities of the mineral springs at **Daylesford**, 27 km (17 miles) north of Creswick. A modern mineral bath offers therapeutic bathing in plain, herbal and bubble baths. For those who wish to "take the waters" internally the naturally effervescent water there is safe and quite palatable.

BENDIGO

Another 80 km (50 miles) north of Ballerat is **Bendigo**, queen city of the goldfields and the greatest field of them all. The riches built a city usually thought of as the best preserved example of late nineteenth century architecture in Victoria. Despite a population of only 50,000 Bendigo boasts two cathedrals, and an art gallery housing one of Australia's finest collections of French Impressionist paintings.

The **Central Deborah Mine**, first worked in the 1850s and closed a century later, has been restored as a working mine museum. A novel way to look about the city is to take the eight kilometer (five mile) ride on the "Talking

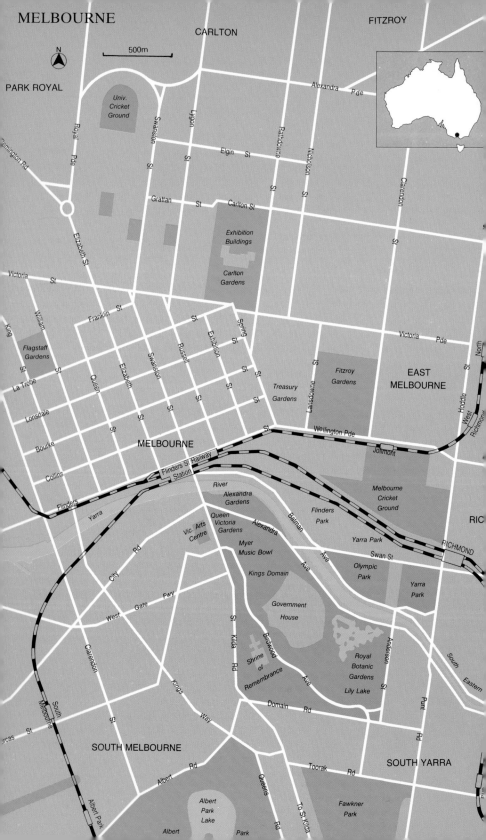

Tram," which runs daily and provides a taped commentary on the attractions along its route.

Arts and Crafts

The reputation of the city's craftsmen is nowhere better established than at Australia's oldest pottery. **Bendigo Pottery** is on the highway and you can see the craftsmen throwing and decorating the pots they sell. A weaving shop in Golden Square demonstrates the skills of spinning and weaving wool.

HOW TO GET THERE

V/Line runs Day Away tours and AAT King's operates a day trip on Fridays to Bendigo and several other old gold towns.

RIVERBOAT ERA

MURRAY RIVER PORTS

The golden days of the riverboats is a chapter often forgotten in Australia's history, but the romance of those adventurous and colorful times lingers on.

Echuca, an hour's drive north of Bendigo through the dairy-rich greenery of the Campaspe Valley, is the patriarch of the great Murray River ports. Just over a century ago, before railroads and decent roads, the Murray was the nation's main trading highway, with hundreds of riverboats plying its 2,590 km (1,610 mile) length. With its tributary, the Darling, it formed a commercial artery for the entire southeast of the continent.

Flourishing, strutting Echuca was the greatest inland port of them all - the second biggest port in Victoria after Melbourne - and its giant triple deck wooden wharf is preserved in the Port of Echuca area. At the turn of the century the town had 80 pubs, and photographs of those days are on display at the His-torical Society's museum.

A dozen or so paddle-wheelers still cruise the river and give visitors a nostalgic ride; other vessels are stationary museums.

The Murray is often little more than a muddy-water trench these days because its waters, controlled by the Snowy Mountains hydro-electric scheme are also siphoned off into irrigation schemes; so it flows only slowly westward towards South Australia, running parallel to the Murray Highway on its southern side.

Half an hour's drive from Echuca the

road passes alongside **Gunbower Island**, a 50 km (31 mile) long bird rookery, and 53 km (33 miles) later reaches **Kerang**, an agricultural town at the end of a chain of lakes which contain some of the largest breeding grounds in the world for ibis and other waterfowl.

At **Swan Hill**, the other great river port of last century, a re-created town of that era is centered around the *Gem*, the biggest and most powerful vessel on the river in its day. The Pioneer Settlement's streets are lined with shops, a smithy, coach offices among other businesses.

Another 250 km (155 miles) downstream is **Mildura**, garden city of the

ABOVE Mildura Post Office.

ver and center of the Sunraysia fruit-growing district.

HOTELS AND MOTELS

Swan Hill Motor Inn, 405 Campbell Street, Swan Hill. Tel: (050) 322726. 59 suites and rooms. Rates: average.
Paruna Motel, 386 Campbell Street, Swan Hill. Tel: (050) 324455. 16 units. Rates: average.

RESTAURANTS

Carriages, Pioneer Motel Inn, 421 Campbell Street, Swan Hill. Good varied menu.
Silver Slipper, Swan Hill Motor Inn, Swan Hill. Ask for the delicious stuffed pork strudel or fresh river fish.

HOW TO GET THERE

V/Line trains run from Melbourne to Swan Hill and a rail/coach service to Echuca. The Vinelander MotoRail runs to Mildura. Coach tours to Echuca are operated by Australian Pacific, and Australian Colonial Tours and Holidaymakers offer extended tours of the Murray region. Greyhound buses bound for Broken Hill pass through Echuca and Swan Hill, and Ansett Pioneer buses to Deniliquin stop at Echuca.

THE GREAT OCEAN ROAD

It's an hour's drive around the western side of Port Phillip Bay to **Geelong,** Victoria's second city and a bustling port and industrial city. Many of its buildings are built of the eye-catching bluestone peculiar to western Victoria.

The coastal route out of Geelong takes you on the 300 km (186 miles) Great Ocean Road, a magnificent ribbon of road which clings to the cliff sides, plunges down to empty bays and swoops around headlands with waves crashing on to rocks just below. For the brief stretches where it strays inland, the road cuts through virtually untouched rain forest, making a pleasant change from the roaring ocean. Its eastern end is on the shore of Bass Strait at the resort of Torquay.

Torquay and other nearby holiday resorts such as **Bells Beach, Anglesea**

RIGHT The whorls of the plough stretch across a corner of the vast wheatlands of Victoria's Wimmera.

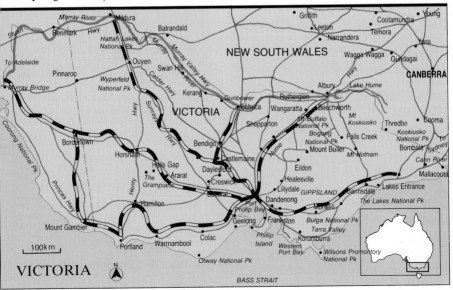

VICTORIA

BASS STRAIT

and **Lorne** have some of the best surf in Australia and the national championships are often held along this stretch of the coast. Lorne has long been a favorite with Melbourne holidaymakers, who are drawn by its old-fashioned charm and by the rain forest hinterland dotted with waterfalls.

Apollo Bay, 48 km (30 miles) west of Lorne, is a picturesque getaway spot which also makes an ideal base for exploring the **Otway Ranges**, known for scenic mountain drives and memorable views over the ocean. After cutting the corner of Cape Otway, the road returns to the coast at Princetown at the eastern end of **Port Campbell National Park**, star attraction of the coastline. Cliffs have been carved by wind and waves into unique formations such as the Twelve Apostles: eroded columns which rear out of the surf and are among the most photographed natural phenomena in Australia.

The Great Ocean Road ends at Peterborough and the route winds westward for another 53 km (32 miles) to **Warrnambool**, a modest-sized city of 20,000. The city guards one of Australia's most intriguing mysteries: the remains of The Mahogany Ship, a Dutch or Spanish vessel which foundered 400 years ago, are believed to lie under the dunes near the old whaling port. Discovery of the wreck would change the history books by indicating that Europeans set foot on the east coast of Australia long before Captain Cook landed. The **Flag Hill Maritime Village** is built around century-old fortifications erected during fears of a Russian invasion.

A short drive along the coast is the rambling little fishing port of **Port Fairy**, which clings to its maritime past and is at the same time a developing holiday resort. Another 70 km (44 miles) around Portland Bay lies **Port-**

ABOVE Fishing boats at Lakes Entrance. RIGHT The coastline worn away to form London Bridge, near Port Campbell.

land, the only deep-water port between Adelaide and Geelong and the location of Victoria's first settlement when the Henty brothers arrived here with their flocks in 1834.

HOTELS AND MOTELS

Richmond Henty Hotel - Motel, 10 Bentinck Street, Portland. Tel: (055) 231032. 45 rooms and units. Rates: average **Selwyns of Sandilands**, 33 Percy Street Portland. Tel: (055) 233319. 4 rooms Rates: budget.

OFF TO GIPPSLAND

The only road out of Melbourne to eastern Victoria leads to a coastline fashioned by nature to a grand design: towering cliffs battered by the sea, networks of tranquil lakes and long, deserted beaches.

The early part of the route is not a scenic wonderland. Although the Princes Highway passes through peaceful green dairy land there are also eyesores in the rm of large open-cut coal mines and their satellite power stations provide the state with its electricity. The Latrobe Valley, the industrial powerhouse of Victoria, is a 60 km (37 mile) seam of coal just below the surface and for most visitors the towns of Moe, Morwell and Traralgon will be signposts on the way.

Drive out of the eastern end of the valley and within less than an hour you are at Sale, the stylish little city which heralds the beginning of the holiday coast of **Gippsland**. It is also the center of the nation's oil and gas industries, and is conveniently near the wells just offshore in the Bass Strait, which meet most of the nation's fuel needs. The story of the oilfield is told in a display center on the highway. Also on the highway is a craft resources center displaying the work of more than 50 local arts and crafts enthusiasts.

Gippsland's fascinating lake system, Australia's largest network of inland lakes, begins just east of Sale. The maze of lakes and lagoons stretches 70 km (44 miles) along the coast behind the protective sand barrier of Ninety Mile Beach and is incredibly beautiful in any season. The shores are dotted with holiday villages. The town of Bairnsdale has a remarkable church with fascinating murals on its walls and ceiling.

The lakes system meets the sea at Lakes Entrance, which in summer is billed as Victoria's leading resort but during the rest of the year is a quiet fishing port. These beautiful lakes are ideal for water sports and facilities are provided so that visitors can sample a variety of them.

The highway east of Lakes Entrance becomes enveloped in the mountains and forests of East Gippsland, and in its remaining 190 km (118 miles) to the New South Wales border passes through only one center of habitation of any size, the timber township of Orbost.

The triangular corner of Victoria is marked by its regal wilderness. The mountains, rain forest, woodlands and rushing rivers are a wonderland for walkers, campers and canoeing enthusiasts. Habitation in this area is confined to hamlets, where people rely on logging or fishing for a living.

HOW TO GET THERE

A bus service to Sydney via the coast road leaves Melbourne daily (the trip takes 18 hours), and major coach companies run extended tours of Gippsland

and the lakes. V/Line terminates at Orbost.

HUME HIGHWAY

Explorers blazed a trail between Sydney and Port Phillip Bay in 1824 and this path is similar to the route now taken by the Hume Highway, the most traveled main road in Australia. The journey through the rolling farmland between Sydney and Melbourne takes about 12 hours.

The road 100 km (62 miles) out of Melbourne passes through the flourishing farming town of Seymour; half-an-hour down the road is the town of **Euroa.** Highlight of the town's Wool Week every November is the valuable Golden Shears sheep-shearing contest.

Benalla, 44 km (27 miles) further on, is known as Rose City because of the thousands of bushes in bloom in public and private gardens from October to April. The modernistic art gallery houses the Ledger of Australian Paintings collection, together with a workshop for painters, spinners and potters.

The highway crosses into New South Wales at the Murray River town of Wodonga. A turn-off at Springsure, just west of Wodonga, leads to **Rutherglen**, heart of another wine-growing area and an enjoyable stopover for a day or two

where you can sample top quality wines, including the Brown Brothers vintages.

NED KELLY

Milestones in the life of Ned Kelly, Australia's most famous outlaw, are strung along the Hume Highway. Arguments continue about whether he was a cowardly killer - he was hanged at the age of 25 for murdering a policeman - or a victim of the times and persecution by police. Dressed in his famous armor he cut a defiant figure in history and i regarded as something of a folk her who was prepared to take a stan against authority.

The Kelly gang's stomping groun stretched south and east of Benalla an Beechworth, and the countryside an towns of Kelly Country retain poignan reminders of the escapades in th 1870s.

The house in which he was born i still to be seen in the village of Beve ridge, and at Avenel he waded int Hughes Creek to rescue a drowning boy Kelly saw the inside of Benalla cour house, and he was imprisoned at Beech worth, the delightful gold rush tow which seems to have changed littl since Kelly's day. The outlaw stage his famous armor-plated final shoot-ou with police at Glenrowan, and the town' souvenir shops see to it that the legen lives on.

HOW TO GET THERE

A frequent bus service runs along th highway and there is a good train serv ice along the line which runs parallel t the road. Coach tours take in Ruther glen vineyards and Kelly Country an are well worth taking to get a first han glimpse of Australia's past.

SKIING AND EXPLORING

THE ALPS

A much less used and more leisurely alternative to the Hume Highway skirts the fringe of the great bulk of the Australian Alps and joins the highway a Benalla.

The Maroondah Highway climbs northeast out of Melbourne towards the high country and **Eildon,** the township near the shores of Lake Eildon. Victoria's largest man-made body of water has a shoreline of 500 km (310 miles), and good trout fishing is to be found here. The road winds around the lake to Mansfield and the turn-off to **Mount Buller,** Victoria's largest ski center.

The scenery up there and all over the alpine high country is breath-takingly beautiful. Peaks climb to more than 2,000 m (6,560 ft), and then plunge away into deep, shadowed valleys. In spring the slopes are brilliant with wildflowers and the quiet is broken only by the sound of tinkling streams. Head north out of Mansfield and you rejoin the highway.

Victoria's other main ski-fields, at **Falls Creek, Mt Buffalo** and **Mt Hotham,** are reached via the Ovens Highway, which turns off the Hume Highway at Wangaratta. The road follows the Ovens River along its broad valley between vineyards, hop fields, walnut groves and tobacco fields. The town of **Bright,** about an hour's drive from Wangaratta, attracts autumn visitors who come to see the oaks and other imported European trees in all their golden glory.

HOW TO GET THERE

Australian Pacific has day tours from Melbourne into the high country, one of which includes a cruise on Lake Eildon.

THE GRAMPIANS

Victoria's only other mountains, the Grampians, form a last thrusting gesture by the Great Dividing Range and are 240 km (150 miles) west of Melbourne. They are the gem of western Victoria's scenery, a collection of steep and craggy peaks 95 km (60 miles) long and 55 km (35 miles) wide, contrasted by the greenery of rainforests and waterfalls. Superb scenic lookouts abound.

More than 1,000 species of native plants have been found there, 200 of them flowering from August to November. Wildlife is abundant and there is also a deer park. **Halls Gap,** focal point of the range, has accommodation and an information office.

HOW TO GET THERE

A daily coach service passes through Ararat, the nearest town to Halls Gap; a three-hour ride. There are also less frequent coach tours from Melbourne. V/Line runs to Ararat.

THE PROM

Wilsons Promontory is about 200 km (125 miles) southeast of Melbourne, an arrow-head pointed at Tasmania across the Bass Strait at Tasmania. It forms one of Victoria's premier national parks, with some of the State's best beaches, and it is best known for the craggy wilderness of its interior and the rugged grandeur of its coast. For hikers there are 80 km (50 miles) of walking tracks in the area.

The most scenic route from Melbourne is along the South Gippsland Highway, which brushes the shore of Western Port Bay and passes through **Korumburra,** a mining village of the 1890s where more than 30 buildings have been authentically restored and reproduced to bring history to life. The mines once provided coal for the railways.

HOW TO GET THERE

The Prom is a very popular attraction and there are coach tours from Melbourne every day.

LEFT Dunes at Croajingolong National Park, which stretches along 38 km (60 miles) of wild coastline.

Queensland

The State That's
Different

People in Brisbane take life at a leisurely pace. Maybe it's the sub-tropical climate, where extravagantly hued blossoms thrive as in a glasshouse but humanity tends to wilt in the summer heat and humidity; possibly it's because this is after all a holiday State; or maybe it's the explanation for Brisbane's atmosphere of a country town. It is only in recent years that Brizzy, as it is nicknamed, has grown up and caught up

with the trend towards high-rise office buildings, freeways and the other trappings of the high-tech age.

The exceptionally large urban area 1,220 sq km (470 sq miles) which houses a million or so residents is laid out on undulating hills which give the city a distinctive dimension. Although the Brisbane River loops through the city it fails to make the same impact on the city as does the Swan on Perth or the Derwent on Hobart. Brisbane's compensation comes 32 km (21 miles) downstream where the river flows into broad Moreton Bay, with its beaches and seaside suburbs.

The abundance of brilliantly colored flowering trees and streets of quaint wooden houses raised on stilts to catch any breezes make Brisbane unique among the capital cities.

In the minds of non-Queenslanders,

Brisbane is the bastion of ultra-conservatism, both socially and politically, and Queenslanders a bunch of "red neck" country crackers who are behind the times. The stubbornly proud Queenslanders, not surprisingly, see themselves and their achievements in a different light.

They believe they are hard-working, virtuous go-getters who pay their way, are beholden to nobody, and succeed through their own achievements - and if the rest of Australia doesn't like their unequivocal way of doing things, too bad.

For all this, the folk of Brisbane - and Queensland - are a personable lot and give a warm welcome to visitors. Brisbane is perhaps less of a tourist destination than other state capitals but is an interesting place to stopover before starting out to explore the attractions of Australia's most exciting holiday State.

THE PAST

Brisbane began its days as a penal settlement and had early setbacks like so many other struggling pioneer encampments. The party of soldiers and intractable convicts sent north from Sydney set up camp on Moreton Bay, only to be harassed by Aborigines. The site also proved to be unsuitable, and the settlement was soon moved up the Brisbane River to the spot where the city center stands today. Moreton Bay District, as Brisbane was then known, was to remain a Sydney-controlled outpost for 35 years before it separated from New South Wales and became a colony in its own right.

Once the hinterland had been opened up, in the face of sometimes bloody opposition from Aborigines, the subsequent rural wealth brought growth to Brisbane. Cattlemen from New South

ABOVE AND RIGHT Australia's favorites entertain the kids at Brisbane's Lone Pine Sanctuary.

Wales drove their herds north to the wide plains and tablelands and took over massive tracts, while the discovery of gold and the beginnings of a mighty sugar industry added to the riches.

Queensland has built up Australia's biggest coal-mining industry from nothing since World War II, and together with the influence of the farming wealth, this gives Brisbane a lot of clout in Australia's economy today. Canberra might not always like what Queensland has to say, but it is obliged to listen.

Tourist Information

The Queensland Government Travel Centre, on the corner of Adelaide and Edward streets, tel: (07) 312211, answers travel queries and can also make bookings. The City Council's Information Centre is at the Albert Street end of Queen Street mall.

TOURING THE CITY

The shopping and business district is confined within one bend of the river.

The symbolic hub of the city is the town hall, once the most notable landmark but now surrounded by glass and concrete towers. From the top of the 91 m (300 ft) clock tower it is still possible to get a bird's-eye view of the central district below. Return to ground level, walk eastward along Ann Street for a couple of blocks and you come to **Anzac Square**, part of a three-block precinct which contains many buildings of historical and architectural significance. The eternal flame of remembrance burns in the circular memorial.

Walk north and within a couple of minutes you are in **Albert Park**, where the Old Windmill is one of the convict-built constructions in the city. It never worked properly as a windmill, so it was equipped with treadmills and powered by wrongdoers. In the 1930s it featured in the nation's first television picture, which was transmitted to Ipswich 40 km (25 miles) away.

Look across the river from the other building erected by convicts, the **Old Commissariat Store** on North Quay, and the eye focuses on the angular shape of the new **Cultural Centre**, with its performing complex, art gallery museum and library. The gallery displays the State's art collection in a building set off by a water mall of fountains and gardens; the theater and concert hall each seat 2,000. Films, poetry, drama readings and other activities are also provided for.

Tours of the complex leave on the hour from 10 am to 4 pm, Monday to Saturday.

Back across the river and you come to Brisbane's most striking edifice (it would be an insult to call it a building) the extravagantly-designed **Treasury**, built a century ago and recognized as the best example of Italian Renaissance architecture in the Southern Hemisphere. It is even more impressive when floodlit, so try to see it at night.

South along George Street lies the

Botanic Gardens, which border the river. The area was first used by convicts for growing vegetables, and the southern tip is still known as Gardens Point. The first director laid out the gardens much as they appear now, and you can still walk down the avenue of bunya pines which he planted. The gardens are popular with Sunday strollers.

SHOPPING

The main shops are to be found in **Queen Street**, part of which has been closed to traffic and converted into an imaginative mall, complete with an information kiosk for visitors.

A rash of redevelopment has resulted in several new shopping plazas, such as the **City Plaza** on the corner of Ann and George streets, which has almost 60 specialty shops and open-air cafés. **Rowes Arcade**, off Post Office Square, has an Edwardian charm. Queensland has its own opal fields and a number of shops in Brisbane specialize in these precious stones.

FURTHER AFIELD

Can anyone resist a cuddly koala? (And by the way they are not "koala bears," just "koalas"). Eleven kilometers (seven miles) upriver at Fig Tree Pocket, live more than 100 of them in the **Lone Pine Koala Sanctuary**. You can have your photograph taken holding one - but watch the claws, they tend to hang on belying the koala's look of innocence. You may stroll through the parkland and feed the kangaroos and emus, and see the hedgehog-like echidnas and chunky barrel-shaped creatures called wombats. A launch leaves Hayles Wharf at North Quay daily at 1:15 pm, with an additional morning departure on Sundays.

If you drive to the sanctuary, the Western Freeway brushes **Mt Coot-tha** and the 57 hectares (140 acres) of botanic gardens being developed at its

foot as the city's "breathing space." Lagoons and ponds are connected by rippling streams, and rain forest and arid zones represent the contrasts to be found in the State. Australia's largest planetarium there presents twice-daily programs Wednesday to Sunday.

The 20-minute drive in from the airport takes you past **Newstead House**, Brisbane's oldest residence. This was the unofficial Government House while it was the home of the Government Resident, the representative of the New South Wales administration before Queensland

became a colony in its own right. The tall column behind the house is a memorial to United States servicemen. Thousands of them were stationed in Brisbane during World War II, and General Douglas MacArthur set up his headquarters in the city for some time before returning to the Pacific.

Moreton Bay, where Brisbane first began life, is a pleasant fringe of quiet

Faces of northern Queensland: LEFT An aboriginal boy in ceremonial paint and ABOVE station hands in rodeo garb.

bay-side villages, beaches and winding channels. Resorts are developing on some islands, and **Moreton, North Stradbroke** and **St Helena** are conveniently accessible. Moreton Island's towering sandhills are claimed to be the world's loftiest and **St Helena** is a national park. Ferries operate to all three islands.

HOW TO GET ABOUT

City Explorer bus tours leave the travel center hourly and make eleven stops along the route, allowing passengers to get off and shop or sight-see and catch another bus later. A number of companies operate half-day and day tours of the city, all leaving from the Government Travel Centre. Hayles operate several river cruises.

BRISBANE BY NIGHT

Despite being thought of by the south

erners as prissy and straight-laced (*Playboy* magazine was banned at one time) Brisbane knows how to kick up its heels come sundown.

Sybils' four floors in Adelaide Street jive until 3 am, and in **Paddington's** Caxton Street there is the **Brisbane Underground**. The Dome Room is for the youngsters, while Downunder is for the over-25s. **Images** makes the world go around on the revolving 24th floor of the GIO building on the corner of Albert and Turbot Street, and **General Jackson's Adult Disco** rages on until 3 am in the Crest International Hotel in Ann Street.

For something more racy, **World By Night** in Queen Street parades a bevy of strippers, and the waitresses are topless too.

Several pubs put on excellent jazz, and the best way to find out who's playing where is through the local newspapers.

There is theater at the **Cultural Centre**, with an active program of productions and concerts, and the **Brisbane Arts Theatre** is in Petrie Terrace.

BELOW The Mall, Brisbane's traffic-free thoroughfare. RIGHT AND OPPOSITE Two of the four bridges which link the center with the south of the city.

Tours By Night

It's all happening on Friday and Saturday evenings. Sunstate Tours take you to a woolshed bush dance or on a nightlife tour, while Hayles operates a cabaret cruise.

HOTELS AND MOTELS

Sheraton-Brisbane Hotel and Towers, 249 Turbot Street. Tel: (07) 835 3535. 441 units and suites. Rates: expensive.

Brisbane Parkroyal, corner Alice and Albert streets. Tel: (07) 221 3411. 173 units and suites. Rates: expensive.

Coronation Motel, 205 Coronation Drive. Tel: (07) 369 9955. 59 units and suites. Rates: moderate.

Gateway Hotel, 85 North Quay. Tel: (07) 221 0211. 191 units and suites. Rates: moderate.

Marrs Town House, 391 Wickham Terrace. Tel: (07) 831 5388. 52 units. Rates: budget.

Yale Budget Inn, 413 Upper Edward Street. Tel: (07) 832 1663. 60 rooms. Rates: budget.

Tourist Private Hotel, 555 Gregory Terrace. Tel: (07) 524171. 37 rooms and units. Rates: budget.

RESTAURANTS

Baguette, 150 Racecourse Road, Ascot. Excellent French cuisine and an international menu.

Banjo Paterson, 791 Old Cleveland Road, Carina. Australian-theme dishes excellently cooked.

The Clansmen, 35 Waldheim Street, Anneley. A converted colonial home with a cellar of more than 10,000 bottles.

Squirrels, 190 Melbourne Street. Vegetarian food presented with imagination at cost-conscious prices.

The Fountain Room, Queensland Cultural Centre, South Brisbane. A beautiful evening setting, looking across the river to the lights of the city. Boned quail in pastry is recommended if it happens to be on the menu.

Fiorini, Caxton Street, Petrie Terrace. A popular trattoria serving traditional Italian dishes. The pastas, in a variety of flavors, are excellent.

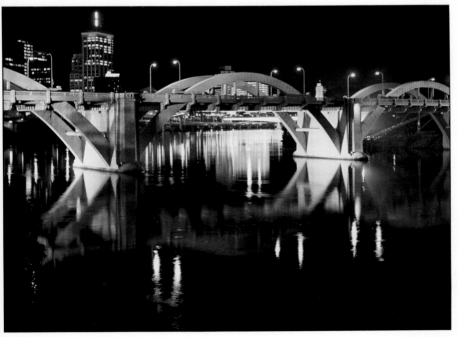

How to Get There

From Sydney, Brisbane is an hour by air, 17 hours by bus and 15 hours by train aboard the Brisbane Limited.

OUT OF BRISBANE

The Gold Coast

An hours's drive south of Brisbane down the Pacific Highway is Australia's version of Miami.

The Gold Coast is the nation's most famous playground. Its 42 km (26 miles) of sun, surf and sand each year attracts more visitors than the population of Queensland.

The big drawcard is **Surfers Paradise**, a dynamic, jazzy and pushy resort of high-rise hotels and apartment towers ranked along the ocean-front Esplanade. Behind it the traffic-clogged main street runs through the middle of town, unable to cope with the explosive development. The creed is "Growth" - knocking something down today and replacing it with something bigger and better tomorrow. The pace of expansion varies between overdrive and frantic.

Networks of canals have been dredged out and the banks lined with smart new homes, with private jetties and boats at the bottom of the gardens. A complete new ocean entrance has been built to attract more sailors and boating people, and man-made harbors have been formed. The building transformation seems ceaseless as more and more people are attracted to "the good life" that the name Surfers Paradise seems to promise.

When the lights go on, Surfers goes into high-gear - restaurants and sidewalks crowd with people looking for some fun. Restaurants proliferate and cater to every taste from take-away to gourmet and for shows there is everything from music hall to dancing girls.

The latest attraction in town is the $175 million **Jupiter's Casino**, a 24-hour gambling hall with a 1,200-seat setting for shows á la Las Vegas, and Jupiter's nightclub. The casino is part of the adjacent Conrads International Hotel, which with 659 rooms is the largest hotel in Australia.

The Coast runs southward as far as the New South Wales border through a succession of smaller resorts which are as slow-paced as Surfers is frenzied. There are all the usual holiday coast attractions - marine parks, amusement parks

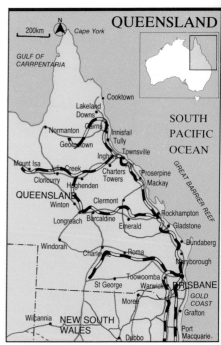

with fairground rides, wildlife sanctuaries, and also waxworks. Two favorites are **Sea World** at Southport, where dolphins jump through hoops and water skiers put on a ballet; and the **Bird Park** at Currumbin, where you can help feed the flocks of brightly colored lorikeets.

Inland, the countryside climbs quickly into the Great Dividing Range and the serene world of rainforest, gorges, orchids and ferns of the incredibly beautiful **Lamington Plateau.** Hundreds of waterfalls tumble over the escarpment and some of the towering Antarctic beech trees are believed to be more than 3,000 years old. An area of 200 sq km (76 sq miles) is set aside as a national park, with many bushwalks and drives ending in lookouts. **Tamborine Mountain** to the north is another national park and is made up of seven areas of jungle where waterfalls cascading down the mountain catch rainbows in their spray.

Touring the Gold Coast
All the coach companies run day-trips

rooms and suites. Rates: expensive.
Chevron Paradise, Ferny Island, Surfers Paradise. Tel: (075) 390444. 347 rooms and suites. Rates: expensive.
Islander Quality Inn, 6 Beach Road, Surfers Paradise. Tel: (075) 388000. 112 rooms and suites. Rates: average.
Paradise Towers Motel, 3051 Gold Coast Highway, Surfers Paradise. Tel: (075) 398488. 80 units. Rates: average.
Surf & Sun, 3323 Gold Coast Highway, Surfers Paradise. Tel: (075) 316481. 16 units. Rates: budget.
Cecil Hotel, 42 Nerang Street, South-

from Brisbane, and Boomerang has a trip just to Jupiter's casino.

Tourist Information
The Government Tourist Bureau on the Gold Coast Highway at Surfers Paradise, tel: (075) 385998 should have the answers to any travel questions.

HOTELS AND MOTELS

Conrad International Hotel, Broadbeach Island. Tel: ((075) 921133. 659

port. Tel: (075) 311031. 11 rooms. Rates: budget.

RESTAURANTS

Eliza's. 199 Cavill Avenue, Surfers Paradise. Don't go beyond the seafood.
Oskars Garden Restaurant, corner Orchard and Elkhorn Avenues, Surfers Paradise. Try the oyster bar.

ABOVE The domes of Australia's largest planetarium in Brisbane's Mt Coot-tha Botanic Gardens.

You and Me, Nelson Building, 4 Admiralty Drive, Paradise Waters. Menu changes monthly.

HOW TO GET THERE

If you don't want to travel all the way by bus, there's always Queensland Railways' Metro-link. The train goes to Beenleigh, where a waiting bus takes you the rest of the way.

A QUIETER COAST

The **Sunshine Coast** lies to the north of Brisbane and is more sedate than its cheeky southern counterpart. Life moves at a gentler pace in **Caloundra, Mooloolaba** and **Maroochydore**, principal resorts along the 56 km (35 mile) string of beaches and rocky headlands. Investment dollars have begun to change the area, but the expansion is unlikely to result in the frenetic atmosphere of the Gold Coast.

All on its own at the northern end of the Coast is **Noosa Heads**, an "in" place of the '80s. A few years ago it was "discovered" by the affluent and trendy people of Sydney and Melbourne and they now call it their own and think of it in terms of a haven from their city lives. The narrow main street, set off with exotic flowering trees, is lined with restaurants serving top-price food and discreet boutiques whose win-

dows shriek money. Just to make sure the city clan do not become too precious, an egalitarian touch is provided by the surfies who come for some of the best waves in Queensland.

The coast has its share of family attractions such as fairytale castles, pioneer villages and a museum; while for something different there is Australia's only ginger factory at Yandina.

Touring the Coast

Sunstate runs a day-long tour on weekdays, and Boomerang puts on a coach every day.

HOW TO GET THERE

Catch a train from Roma Street station in Brisbane and get off at Nambour, then take a taxi the remaining 18 km (11 miles). Skennars Coaches operate the Sunshine Coast-Brisbane service and pick up passengers at Brisbane airport. Flights from Maroochydore airport connect at Brisbane with interstate planes.

BOUNTIFUL DARLING DOWNS

Before he could discover what were to become Queensland's richest farming lands, explorer Allan Cunningham had to slog over the Great Dividing Range through the Gap which now bears his name and up on to the rich blacksoil plains of the Darling Downs west of Brisbane. Life is less tedious a century and a half later; it's a comfortable 140 km (90 mile) ride of less than two hours by road or rail from Brisbane to the main center of the Downs, **Toowoomba**.

With its tree-lined streets and beautifully tended parks and gardens it is obvious why Toowoomba has earned the sobriquet The Garden City. Highlight of the year is the Carnival of Flowers

OPPOSITE Flower power and shopping for Gold Coast seafood. ABOVE A king-size chess game at Surfers Paradise.

every September, when thousands of Australian and overseas visitors flock to the city.

But Toowoomba doesn't spend all its time tending the flowers. The wealth of the Downs has seen it grow into Queensland's largest inland city (pop. 67,000) and it has become the headquarters for farmers of the rich, manicured farmland which stretches beyond the flat horizon and each year produces cattle, sheep, wheat, cotton and other crops worth hundreds of millions of dollars.

Queensland's largest woolshed, on **Jondaryan** station 40 km (25 miles) along the Warrego Highway, has been turned into a working museum where you can watch the shearers and smithy at work.

HOW TO GET THERE

Queensland Railways run to Toowoomba. There is also a Metro-link service to Ipswich, at the end of the suburban line, where you can connect with a bus tour. Coach companies run day-trips to the Downs.

UNDERWATER WONDERLAND

There's only one **Great Barrier Reef** in the world. And it really is one of the world's natural wonders, set in the tropical paradise as portrayed in posters and postcards, with crystal-clear seas, turquoise skies and delightful scenic islands.

Stretching for 1,930 km (1,200 miles) along the coast as far south as Bundaberg, it is nature's biggest living organism; created by a myriad of tiny coral polyps each no larger than a pinhead, whose skeletons have built up layer upon layer over thousands of years.

The outer reef lies from between 25 km (15 miles) to 400 km (250 miles) offshore, and the lagoon formed by it is an underwater kaleidoscope of color and movement. An estimated 1,400 species

of fish, many as brilliant as jewels, glide between waving sponges and delicate coral formations, as fragile starfish and urchins ruminate among the grottoes. The true beauty of the reef lies below the surface, so if you are not a scuba diver (some resorts give lessons), at least invest in a snorkel and flippers so that you can look through your own window into this remarkable world. If you feel that even snorkeling is a bit beyond you, join a glass-bottom boat tour and see sights the easy way.

If you're expecting all the 250 is-

lands to be like something out of the South Seas - low-lying coral cays fringed with long beaches and crowned by waving palms - you are in for a shock.

Only a handful of islands are cays, and only two of these, **Heron Island**, 70 km (45 miles) off Gladstone, and **Green Island**, 27 km (16 miles) from Cairns, have facilities for visitors. All the other islands have no connection with coral; they are the tops of mounains separated from the mainland, and ise abruptly out of the water, most of hem covered with thick vegetation. Many are national parks.

About a score of islands have holiday facilities, with the main concentration of resorts congregating on islands bordering the Whitsunday Passage, north of Mackay.

Big money is being poured into upgrading the Whitsunday Islands. And with talk of multi-million dollar projects, hotels being built on the seabed and other schemes, conservationists are

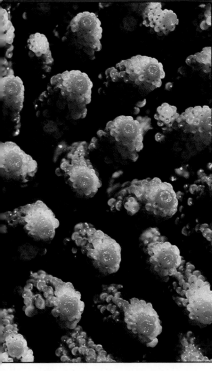

expressing concern over whether the ecology can withstand the pressure created by a large influx of visitors. One costly development has already had to be abandoned because of public reaction, and others may follow as conservationists step up the fight to preserve the Reef's natural beauty.

Hamilton Island is the fastest developing of the Whitsunday group, and apart from 14-story condominiums also has 170 lodges, smaller condominiums, and a landing strip large enough for medium-size jets arriving direct from Sydney and Brisbane.

This brief summary of a few of the islands is listed south to north:

Heron Island: A coral cay showpiece, only 16 hectares (40 acres) at low tide, ringed by superb coral flats. The island is also a turtle rookery, and between September and January you can watch females laying their eggs in scrapes on the beach. Superb diving and snorkeling.

Great Keppel Island: A resort off Rockhampton catering for the young folk. Water skiing, parasailing and other activities by day, discoing by night. Choose from 17 beaches.

Lindeman Island: A hilly island with a family resort at the southern end of Whitsunday Passage. An adventure camp for the kids, golf course for parents, and an air service to Mackay and to Proserpine.

Hamilton Island: You name it, they've got it.

South Molle Island: The resort has been upgraded, and the activities blackboard is daunting. A short ride from Shute Harbour, the main jumping-off point for the Whitsunday Passage.

Hook Island: Excellent coral flats

ABOVE Some of the varieties of coral on the Great Barrier Reef. About 350 species are to be found.

and an underwater observatory where the fish swim up to take a look at you, but little in the way of accommodation.

Hayman Island: Re-opened after a $25 million redevelopment, the Whitsunday resort sits on the island's only flat area and looks out over a lagoon.

Green Island: A coral cay just off Cairns; worth a visit for the underwater observatory.

Lizard Island: Most northerly of the resorts, 90 km (50 miles) north of Cooktown. The outer reef is only 15 km (10 miles) away and it is possible to watch waves pounding the edge of the continental shelf as far as the eye can see. A base for marlin fishermen during the October-November season.

TOURING THE REEF

Launches and big catamarans leave daily from Mackay, Airlie Beach and the main embarkation point for the Whitsunday Islands, Shute Harbour. A visit to the Reef is on many long-distance coach tours.

HOW TO GET THERE

The best time to go is between April and October. Contact the Government Tourist Office for the most convenient hopping-off point to the various islands, some of which can be reached by air. It's about 22 hours by train from Brisbane to Proserpine, nearest rail town to the Whitsundays.

THE BRUCE HIGHWAY: GOING TROPPO

BLOSSOMS, RUM AND COWS

There's only one good road to the north, the Bruce Highway which stretches 1,841 km (1,150 miles) along the coast from Brisbane to Cairns. It's a very scenic route, through chequer boards of sugar cane from which palls of smoke rise in the latter part of the year during pre-cutting burn-offs. The highway passes through towns of fancily decorated wooden houses raised on stilts, glowing with bougainvillea and other blossoms. The ever-present Great Dividing Range is on the left-hand side covered in dense rain forest and in the far north often topped by brooding rain clouds. Along the coast are an endless succession of beaches, seashore villages and the atmosphere is laid-back and relaxed.

The highway runs through its first cane fields at **Nambour**, an hour north of Brisbane, and the distinctive rich green rectangles will be a feature of the scenery all the way to Cairns and beyond - visible evidence of Australia's position as the world's fourth largest sugar producer.

Bundaberg is toasted by rum drinkers around Australia for its "Bundy" rum, a hearty dark rum which comes from a distillery attached to one of the city's five sugar mills. The refinery and distillery are open to the public during the July-December crushing season, as is the world's longest sugar storage shed - the length of four football fields. To reach Bundaberg take a 50 km (35 mile) detour off the highway; it is about three hours by road out of Brisbane.

Another 270 km (168 miles) north at **Rockhampton** you officially enter the tropics - or almost. The Tropic of Capricorn spire by the roadside at the city entrance was erected on the tropical latitude, but was then moved when the highway was realigned. "Rocky" is Queensland's biggest cow town, with tens of thousands of head each year being shipped to the abattoirs and packing plants. About one-third of the State's cattle graze on stations within 250 km (155 miles) of the city.

A handsome Customs House is one of 50 National Trust-registered buildings along Quay Street, an elegant avenue along the banks of the Fitzroy River.

HOTELS AND MOTELS

Duthies Leichhardt Hotel, corner Bolsover and Denham Streets, Rockhampton. Tel: (079) 276733. 120 rooms and suites. Rates: average.
Fountain Motor Inn, 161 George Street, Rockhampton. Tel: (079) 275855. 73 units. Rates: average.
Al Motel, Main Street, Rockhampton.

Tel: (079) 242551. 17 units. Rates: budget.

CANE AND CROCODILES

A quarter of the Australian sugar crop is grown in the sea of cane fields surrounding **Mackay**, 340 km (210 miles) to the north. Royal palms and tall blossom trees line its broad streets. **Queen's Park**, a showpiece of palms and exotic blooms, also houses a fern and orchid

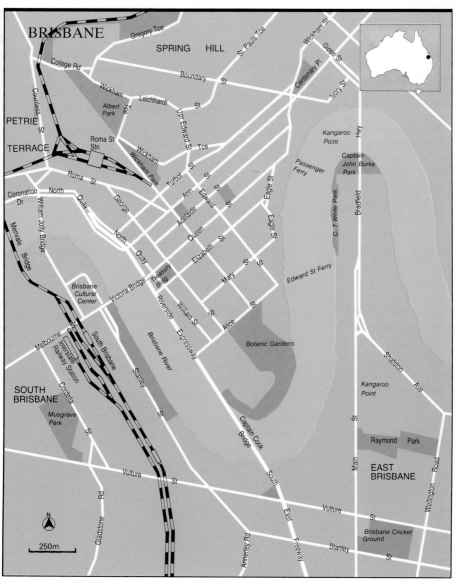

conservatory. Visitors approaching from the south may be surprised by the incongruous sight of a beached Vietnamese fishing vessel mounted by the side of the highway. The vessel was confiscated for fishing in Australian waters, and is now the city's information center, tel: (079) 522038.

Eungella National Park, mountainous, often mist-shrouded and 45 minutes' drive west of Mackay, takes its name from the local Aboriginal word for "Land of Cloud." The sound of water is ever present, as sparkling creeks splash over rocks and plunge down inaccessible mountain slopes into deep ravines. Trees are festooned with ferns which thrive in the damp atmosphere. There are 25 km (15 miles) of walking tracks in the park for those who want to take a closer look at its scenic beauty.

Proserpine, 130 km (81 miles) north of Mackay, is the turn-off for Shute Haroour, departure point for the Whitsunday Passage islands.

Crocodiles were sunning themselves on the bank of Ross Creek when the first settlers arrived to establish **Townsville**. Today, only 120 years later, the city is the third largest in Queensland and the main center of population of the north. Visitors get the best view from Castle Hill, a 300 m (985 ft) red granite outcrop, which rises immediately behind the business center. The vantage point looks down upon a city which is still growing, but which has managed to retain much of its colonial elegance.

Across Cleveland Bay lies **Magnetic Island**, part national park and part suburb, only a 40-minute ferry ride away.

The bay is fringed by **The Strand**, an attractive esplanade with tropical gardens, floodlit waterfall and masses of overhanging bougainvillea. At the northern end is a memorial to those who fought in the Battle of the Coral Sea; the airport was a base for operations during that battle. James Cook University, Australia's only university in the tropics, is prominent in its field of research into marine biology and veterinary subjects.

Well worth a visit is the **Town Common**, a reserve which is the home of hundreds of species of birds and reptiles. Many of the birds are migratory, and flocks of brolgas, Australia's only species of crane, also winter here. A visit to **Queens Gardens** with its ornamental lakes, tropical trees and flowers is a visual delight.

The sugar cane plantations seem to continue endlessly to the north of

Townsville, aided by abundant rain, for this is the wettest patch of the continent. Tully has the singular honor of being the rainiest place in Australia, with a yearly average rainfall of 4,490 mm (175 inches), most of it falling between late November and March, the season of the Wet.

HOTELS AND MOTELS

Townsville International Hotel, Flinders Mall, Townsville. Tel: (077) 722477. 124 units. Rates: expensive.
Travelodge, the Strand, Townsville. Tel: (077) 724255. 153 units and suites.

Rates: average.
Bessell Lodge, Bundock Street, Belgian Gardens. Tel: (077) 725055. 53 units. Rates: average.
Allen Hotel, corner Gregory and Eyre Streets, Townsville. Tel: (077) 715656. 50 rooms. Rates: budget.
Civic Guest House, 262 Walker Street, Townsville. Tel: (077) 715381. 23 rooms. Rates: budget.

CAIRNS

Cairns, the last stop of any size up the coast, is a half-day's drive beyond Townsville, and is a casual and colorful waterfront city. The main rail line ends here and so does the Bruce Highway. Life here is lived at a leisurely pace taking its cue from the heat and humidity. In summer it is fragrant from the frangipani and bougainvillea with poinciana ablaze with color.

Cairns is best known as the home port of the Marlin Meet, when game fishermen from all parts of the world congregate to hunt for the huge black marlin that cruise south on their annual migration along the ocean side of the Great Barrier Reef. Many fishermen come in their own boats for the event, and the season lasts from September to December. Landlubbers can watch the marine monsters being weighed in at the official station at the mouth of Trinity Inlet.

The city is an ideal base for touring. Launches leave for Green Island, 27 km (16 miles) out to sea, while Australia's most heart-stopping railroad ride can take you inland and upward to the **Atherton Tableland**, a plateau of rolling farmland and sharp, broken ranges.

The track clings to the face of the escarpment and winds through 15 tunnels and over almost 40 bridges. Passengers can almost reach out and touch tumbling waterfalls. The train travels past the edge of Barron Falls, which in spate is a thundering torrent which plunges hundreds of meters into a gorge colored with rainbow-flecked spray.

The road to the isolated village of **Cooktown**, 180 km (110 miles) up the coast, takes a short cut through dripping rainforest. The construction of this road in the early 1980s brought conservationists out in force – protestors even lay down in front of bulldozers to try to stop the road-builders; the State government refused to make any concessions and the road was eventually completed.

Cooktown was Australia's first white settlement, in 1770 – if only temporarily. James Cook beached his vessel *Endeavor* for repairs after it was damaged on the Great Barrier Reef. A century later the town had a population of 30,000 and a main street two kilometers long when it was the port for an up-country gold rush that has since subsided.

Touring from Cairns
Bus tours take visitors to the rainforest and national parks on the tableland. For those intrepid souls who want to trek another 1,300 km (800 miles) northward to Cape York it's essential to know it is a hard four-day safari trek in a four-wheel drive along a track impassable in the rainy season.

Tourist Information
The Government Tourist Bureau in Abbott Street, tel: (070) 514066, has details of all tours.

HOTELS AND MOTELS

Pacific International, 143 The Esplanade, Cairns. Tel: (070) 517888. 176 rooms. Rates: expensive.
Tuna Lodge, 127 The Esplanade, Cairns. Tel: (070) 514388. 62 units. Rates: average.

OPPOSITE Flocks of rainbow lorikeets fly in to be fed by visitors to Currumbin sanctuary on the Gold Coast.

Tradewinds Sun Lodge, corner Lake and Florence streets, Cairns. Tel: (070) 515733. 65 units. Rates: average.

How to Get There

The Sunlander sleeper train leaves Brisbane's Roma Street station at breakfast time and arrives in Cairns at teatime the following day. The Capricornian, a more leisurely daylight rail tour which takes six days to cover the same distance, stops overnight along the line and for sightseeing trips. The Sunlander train from Brisbane takes seven hours to Bundaberg, 13 hours to Rockhampton, 20 hours to Mackay, 27 hours to Townsville and 34 hours to Cairns

The major coach companies run multi-day tours along the Bruce Highway and there is a regular daily service along the route. It's an hour by air from Brisbane to Rockhampton, 1 hour 45 minutes to Townsville and 2 hours 45 minutes to Cairns.

Off the Beaten Track

Virtually everything away from the Bruce Highway and southeast corner of the State, where half the 2.3 million Queenslanders live, is off the beaten track in this far-flung region of the continent. Even some of the major highways and through roads have dirt surfaces, and minor roads in the Outback are little more than tracks. Roads in the northern inland, apart from the highways, can be impassable in the wet season, and in the Channel Country of the flat southwest, flooded rivers can become many kilometers wide.

The interior is a semi-arid sea of spinifex and spindly mitchell grass that shimmers in the summer heat and burns red at sunset. Isolated cattle stations keep in touch with the world by radio, and townships are hundreds of kilometers apart. Smaller only than the mining city of Mt Isa, the second largest town in the Outback, is Charleville, with a population of 3,500.

Detours Off the Bruce

While traveling along the coast, make time to stray from the highway – you will find the detours enjoyable.

By turning off at Maryborough, you can catch a ferry at Hervey Bay for **Fraser Island**, the world's largest sand island. The 1,550 sq km (600 sq mile) island supports large areas of forest interspersed with towering dunes, and teems with wildlife such as kangaroos, wild horses and dingoes. There are several resorts if you want to stay a few days and explore the island at your leisure

A half-hour drive east of Rockhampton, the Capricorn Coast is a string of small resorts stretching for 25 km (15 miles) along pleasant tree-lined beaches.

One of the biggest holes dug by man is at **Mt Morgan**, a former gold mining town 40 km (25 miles) out of "Rocky". The open-cut mine gave more than five million ounces of gold before its seams were exhausted.

Coach tours of the Capricorn Coast depart from Rockhampton, and a bus leaves the post office at 8 am to catch the daily cruise to the resort island of Great Keppel.

If you happen to be excited by coal-loading terminals, the world's largest is to be found at **Hay Point**; the turn-off is signposted a few kilometers south of Mackay. The installation can ship 40 million tons a year, which arrives from inland mines in trains two kilometers long.

Residents were once so proud of the bonanza gold mining town of **Charters Towers**, 130 km (85 miles) along the Mt Isa road from Townsville, that they called it The World. The stock exchange has been restored to the splendor of the

OPPOSITE Waiting for a bite on the Norman River, which flows into the Gulf of Carpentaria.

days when it was the nerve center of Queensland's most productive gold town. It survives – unlike most former gold towns – as a place of modern charm and Victorian dignity, having replaced gold with farming. Standard White Cabs of Townsville will operate day tours to Charters Towers.

THE ISA

To the world outside Queensland it's called a town which exists solely for the riches mined there. Here is the world's largest single-mine producer of lead and silver, and Queensland's biggest single industrial enterprise.

The city did not exist before 1923, when a prospector found a mineral outcrop, and in time it led to the formation of a remote city surrounded by harsh country. An underground tour of the mine is available to visitors and gives a fascinating insight into the difficulties still encountered in modern mining.

HOW TO GET THERE

Mount Isa is an interesting stopover on flights between Brisbane and Darwin and is also on the route of the coach tours which take in the Northern Territory. The city can also be reached by train from Townsville, 930 km (580 miles) to the east, though the journey takes about 20 hours. By comparison, a daily bus service from Townsville takes 10-1/2 hours.

HOME OF WALTZING MATILDA

Four hundred and fifty kilometers (280 miles) south of Mount Isa along the Landsborough Highway, **Winton** looks just as hot and just as dry as any other small Outback town, but it holds a special place in Australian hearts. The nation's unofficial national anthem, "Waltzing Matilda", had its genesis here. Poet and writer A. B. "Banjo" Paterson was told the true story he later related in the song while visiting the district. The song was first sung in public in the North Gregory Hotel, where the chorus and an illustration of a swagman, an itinerant rural worker, are etched into the door.

Australia's tribute to its Outback pioneers is the **Stockmen's Hall of Fame** and **Outback Heritage Centre** being built at Longreach, 180 km (100 miles) south of Winton. The biggest town in the far west, **Longreach** is the center of a vast cattle and sheep grazing area, and a vital trucking center. When driving in the Outback it is essential to keep a weather eye open for the leviathan road trains which travel the inland roads shipping cattle to and fro. The front truck can be pulling up to three trailers and because of the often narrow roads extreme care must be taken when passing or overtaking them.

Australia's international airline, Qantas (Queensland and Northern Territory Aerial Services) began its flights from Longreach as a three-man rural plane service and the airline's first hangar can still be seen at the airport.

HOW TO GET THERE

In spite of their remoteness (Longreach is 965 km or 600 miles from Brisbane as the crow flies) Longreach and Winton have air and rail services and a daily coach service. Be prepared for a long ride – this really is Outback country. The Midlander train runs between Rockhampton, Longreach and Winton twice a week; 15 hours to Longreach, 20 hours to Winton. The Rockhampton-Longreach bus takes nine hours and is therefore better suited to those with a limited amount of time.

Beach life. TOP LEFT Clifton Beach, near Cairns. TOP RIGHT Mission Beach. BOTTOM Surfers Paradise.

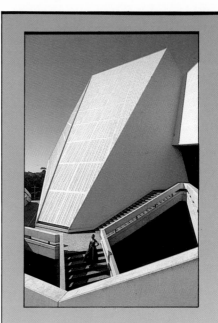

South Australia

State of Elegance

ADELAIDE

The South Australian capital exudes an air of dignity and respectability, while at the same time it gives the feeling of a city that enjoys the better things of life such as good food and wine. It has a casual, unpretentious sense of style which is difficult to find anywhere else in Australia – even in Sydney. It also stages with imagination and panache the best arts festival in Australia.

Lately Adelaide has kicked up her

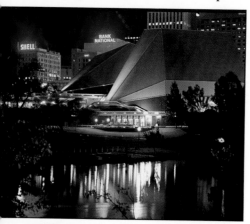

heels and shown a bolder side to her character, converting the railroad station into an elegant European-style casino, and building a highly praised and thrilling motor racing circuit through the city streets, which has been awarded a place on the international grand prix motor racing calendar.

But Adelaide's prime asset stems not from anything contemporary, but from its very foundation. In 1836 the fledgling colony's chief planner, Surveyor-General William Light, laid out a city years ahead of its time. Nothing could be more simple than his orderly grid system exactly one mile square and bordered on the northern side by the twisting River Torrens. Across the river is Light's equally well-planned residen-

tial precinct of North Adelaide.

Surrounding it all is Light's masterstroke, 668 hectares (1,650 acres) of parkland which are now more jealously guarded than anything else in the city.

The result is that 150 years later Adelaide can still cop with its traffic, a rare achievement. A town planner of world repute once commented that the three most charmingly planned cities in the world were Washington, Edinburgh and Adelaide.

Beyond Light's green belt the city stretches to the low sand dune shore of Gulf St Vincent in the west and up into the green folds of the Adelaide Hills to the east.

THE PAST

Adelaide came into being as a semi-independent province under the control of a London-based private company. The concept, radically different from the other colonies, was to fail after six years because of financial collapse, and the enterprise was given the status of a government colony. But Adelaide – like South Australia – holds a special place in Australia's history of white settlement as it was settled entirely by free men, not by convicts.

Extensive copper finds in the 1840s enhanced Adelaide's importance, while the setting up of a rural economy saw it develop as an administrative city. Later it was to become an important manufacturing center, particularly for motor vehicles, enabling it to weather a succession of slumps and booms in the State's agricultural industry.

Like every other Australian city, Adelaide has mushroomed since World War II and with the steady influx of migrants its present population of over 900,000 is double that of 1946.

Tourist Information
The South Australian Government

ABOVE Adelaide Festival Centre, home of the best arts festival in the country.

Travel Centre is at 18 King William Street, tel: (08) 212164, between North Terrace and Rundle Mall. The staff can supply you with information and brochures, and make bookings.

TOURING ADELAIDE

Light's design makes Adelaide a walkers' delight, so after coming out of the Travel Centre, turn the corner and walk along Adelaide's most charming boulevard, **North Terrace**. Along its dignified tree-lined length are South Australia's seats of political power, learning and culture; its heritage.

Government House stands closed to public eyes behind its walls and trees, but head eastward and you can wander past – and drop into if you wish – the **State Library**, the **South Australian Museum** (which houses the world's largest collection of Aboriginal artifacts), and the **Art Gallery of South Australia**. The **University of Adelaide** is cramped between North Terrace and the river, but the overcrowding has not robbed the predominantly Gothic styled

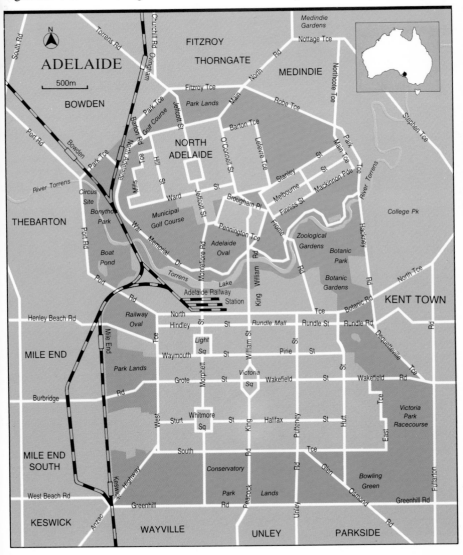

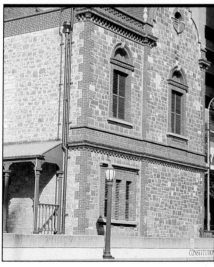

TOP and LEFT Outdoor art at Adelaide's Festival Centre. ABOVE The former State Parliament House now houses the only museum of political history in Australia.

campus of its charms and academic repose. Across the street, **Ayers House** was the home of a seven-time Premier after whom the world's largest monolith, Ayers Rock, is named. Now it houses the headquarters of the State's National Trust, as well as two restaurants.

The **Botanic Gardens**, a relaxing 30 hectares (75 acres) of shady lawns and artificial lakes, leads to the banks of the Torrens and the rural setting makes the city seem far away.

The riverside stroll leads to the **Festival Centre**, core of Adelaide's cultural life. The superbly designed complex houses the Festival Theatre, an experimental theater, the Playhouse, an amphitheater for outdoor performances, and a plaza for informal cultural gatherings such as for poetry readings.

Just behind the Centre stands Adelaide's most handsome building, **Parliament House**; and next door is Australia's only museum of political history, the **Constitutional Museum**, where you can trace the history of the State.

King William Street, backbone of Light's city and at 42 m (140 ft) the widest of any Australian city thoroughfare, slashes across the parkland and river to North Adelaide, where the quiet streets laid out by Light complement his business and administrative district across the Torrens. The suburb is surrounded by its own green space, which takes in the university playing fields, a golf course and a Test ground which many cricket followers ˎconsider the world's prettiest.

Few visitors miss a chance to ride on Adelaide's only streetcar service, a 20-minute trip to the beach suburb of **Glenelg**, where South Australia officially began and which is the most popular destination for a pleasant day by the sea. The gnarled Foundation Tree, beside which the proclamation was read in 1836, has long-since died, but cement and man's ingenuity hold it together to commemorate the occasion.

SHOPPING

Adelaide was the first Australian city to ban vehicles from a main shopping street, and **Rundle Mall** is a bustling pedestrians - only heart to the shopping blocks. It is lined with department stores, dainty boutiques, coffee shops and cinemas. Colorful flower stalls, street entertainers, a fountain and an outdoor restaurant add to its attractiveness. Half a dozen arcade complexes lead off the mall for those seeking even greater shopping variety.

Melbourne Street in North Adelaide has become a lively avenue of trendy restaurants, boutiques and gift shops. The Central Market, in Grote Street, is a noisy, friendly bazaar.

ARTS AND CRAFTS

Adelaide supports a lively group of craftsmen. Turn a corner and more than likely you will come across a gallery or a shop displaying the work of local artists in ceramics, sculpture, pottery, weaving, glassware or prints. The **Jam Factory**, in Payneham Road, an extension of North Terrace, is a government project promoting local arts and crafts.

Antique hunters should head for **Unley Road** or nearby **King William Road**, in Hyde Park, both on the southern edge of the city. And you never know what treasure you may come across at the antique markets at **59 Pultenet Street** and **32 Grote Street**.

How to Get About

The Freeline free bus service runs from Victoria Square, the most central of Adelaide's five squares, and Premier Roadlines and Ansett Pioneer run morning tours. The Adelaide Explorer leaves at 90-minute intervals from the Government Travel Centre.

ADELAIDE BY NIGHT

Hindley Street, where excellent ethnic

restaurants are interspersed with bars, a movie house complex, strip clubs such as the long-running **Crazy Horse**, and adult bookshops, is Adelaide's liveliest street after dark. The **Rio International**, with its piano bar and disco, is open 24 hours a day. **Jules Bar,** a long-running hotspot, is in the Princess Victoria Hotel. **New York, New York**, a disco attached to the Braested Restaurant in Greenhill Road, Parkside, is the one in which to gyrate into the small hours.

There are few cuisines unrepresented in the city that boasts it has more restaurants in proportion to its population than any other city in Australia, but the whiting is an Adelaide specialty and the seafood is superb.

The cultural scene is obviously at its best during the biennial festival, but the Festival Centre is also busy around the year with symphony and pop concerts, theater and other stage shows. Several other theaters such as the **Opera Thea-**

Each big city has its pedestrians-only shopping malls. OPPOSITE Adelaide. LEFT and ABOVE Perth.

tre in Grote Street and the **Arts Theatre** in Angas Street, are well supported and it is worth checking what is on.

Tours By Night

Ansett Pioneer and Premier Roadlines lay on trips to vantage points in the Hills to view the city lights – an excellent way of spending an evening.

ADELAIDE HILLS

William Light called the Hills "the enchanted hills." Narrow, leafy lanes meander around the slopes, brushing close to pretty villages and orchards. A scenic drive along Summit Road is clearly marked, with the favorite lookout of **Mt Lofty** giving a view over the entire city. City families have moved into the Hills in search of rural peace and this influx has been absorbed without any loss of charm.

Most picturesque of the villages is **Hahndorf**, Australia's oldest German settlement – its half-timbered buildings could be right out of a picture book of Germany. There's a German cake shop; an old flour mill now a restaurant specia-

lizing in German cooking; a market place with a European atmosphere, and a smithy-turned-craft shop. **Lobethal** is another village settled by early German migrants and it is also well worth a visit.

Highlight of any day in the Hills is a visit to **Cleland Conservation Park**, on the slopes of Mt Lofty. Here you can walk close to the animals in the large paddocks. As far as possible, animals in each enclosure come from the same habitat, and include koalas, dingoes, wombats, emus, tortoises and a dozen varieties of kangaroos and wallabies.

HOW TO GET THERE

Day tours and half-day tours explore the Hills.

HOTELS AND MOTELS

Hilton International, 233 Victoria Square. Tel: (08) 217 0711. 402 rooms and suites. Rates: expensive.
Gateway Hotel, 147 North Terrace. Tel: (08) 217 7552. 226 rooms and suites. Rates: expensive.
Meridien Lodge Motel, 21 Melbourne

Street, North Adelaide. Tel: (08) 267 3033. 42 rooms and suites. Rates: average.

Telford Old Adelaide Inn, corner O' Connell and Gover Streets, North Adelaide. Tel: (08) 267 5066. Rates: average.

Town House Motel, corner Hindley and Morphett Streets. Tel: (08) 211 8255. 68 units. Rates: average.

Newmarket Hotel, corner West and North Terraces. Tel: (08) 211 8533. 12 rooms. Rates: budget.

Strathmore Hotel, 129 North Terrace. Tel: (08) 51 4456. 20 rooms. Rates: budget.

RESTAURANTS

The Barn, Main Road, McLaren Vale. Serves everything from roast meat to grilled whiting. You enter through an art gallery.

The Contented Sole, 354 Shepherds Hill Road, Blackwood. Combines French flavors with Japanese presentation.

Ettore, 308 Port Road, Hindmarsh. A selection of northern Italian cooking.

The Grange, Hilton International. Very elegant; good international menu.

Henry Ayers House, North Terrace. Possibly the grandest of Adelaide's eateries.

Neddys, 170 Hutt Street. Dishes from northern China, many of them unusual.

Ruby's Cafe, 255b Rundle Street. Small but imaginative menu.

HOW TO GET THERE

Adelaide is now a stop on international flights and a major center on internal routes. Long-distance trains are the Overland to Melbourne (12 hours), the Ghan to Alice Springs (24 hours), and the Trans Australian to Perth (42 hours). Buses go to Alice Springs (26 hours), Melbourne (11 hours), Adelaide (23 hours) and Perth (35 hours).

AN ARID STATE

The landscape around Adelaide is made up of green hills and good farming land, and this can easily give the visitor a false impression of South Australia. Nature has been kind to the south but the northern two-thirds is Outback desert: stony, barren plains where the earth is baked and cracked by the searing heat and hot winds from inland. The land is inhospitable and it's dry. South Australia is the driest State in Australia and the empty northeast corner the most arid part of the continent, rarely receiving more than 120 mm (five inches) of rain a year.

THE BAROSSA VALLEY

The broad 30 km (19 mile) long valley, an hour's drive north of Adelaide, is Australia's best-known wine growing area and producer of some of its most individualistic wines. German Lutherans fleeing persecution 140 years ago settled the valley, and the roots of their heritage are now as firmly planted as the vines whose rows make ruler-straight patterns across the valley floor. The architecture is reminiscent of German towns and villages, and Silesian names hang above shops which sell *leiberwurst* and rich *tortes*, and the many churches have a Lutheran austerity.

Tanunda still has its old marketplace, Zeigenmarkt, ringed with cottages built in a style that was common in Germany when the early settlers arrived, and traditional games such as German skittles are still favorite pastimes. A few kilometers to the west you can walk down the shady main street of **Bethany**, the valley's oldest village, and pass thatched barns and pretty rustic cottages of an earlier romantic era.

The 30-odd wineries add as much to the fascination of the valley as do the villages; many are built to resemble flamboyant medieval chateaux and cas-

OPPOSITE Evening light mellows a Barossa Valley cemetery which contains the graves of German pioneers.

tles. But they are not just pretty facades - they yield a quarter of the national vintage, producing some superb reds and white wines. Every other year harvest time in late summer climaxes in a festival which attracts visitors from all over Australia and from overseas. Many wineries are open to the public and offer interesting and informative tours.

HOW TO GET THERE

There's a day tour every day from Adelaide, and some Sydney-bound buses

stop at Nuriootpa in the heart of the valley.

THE ROAD SOUTH

The Fleurieu Peninsula, to the south of Adelaide, is a coastal vacation area for South Australians. The road out of the city glides through the vineyards of the Southern Vales and along the coast through sleepy little towns which a century ago did much of their business at night, quietly. Smugglers seeking to outwit the Customs men silently landed

cargoes of tobacco and spirits, and everyone kept the secret. Many a group of contraband runners has rowed its illegal merchandise up the Onkaparinga River and hidden over in Noarlunga, where the old Horseshoe Inn was a favorite cache.

Unofficial capital of the peninsula **Victor Harbour**, a resort 84 km (52 miles) out of Adelaide, began as a whaling station and some of its colorful and adventurous past is depicted in the Whalers' Haven Museum. A causeway connects the town to **Granite Island**, reserve for fairy penguins and kangaroos, where a chair lift hauls visitors to the top.

A quarter-hour drive along the coast is **Goolwa**, a drowsy little township near the mouth of the Murray which more than a century ago was a thriving transfer port for river cargoes. Reminders of Australia's first commercial railway, used for railing cargoes to an ocean wharf some kilometers away, are still to be seen, and pride of place goes to the nation's oldest railroad coach, a primitive windowless wooden-bench affair which now sits resplendent in a glass case in the center of town.

HOW TO GET THERE

Day tours leave Adelaide on Wednesday, Thursday, Friday and Sunday.

THE COORONG

South Australia's most fascinating coastline lies to the southeast of Adelaide, along the Princes Highway which leads on to Victoria and Melbourne.

The highway east through the Adelaide Hills crosses the Murray at Murray Bridge and in another 110 km (62 miles) arrives at the windswept beauty of The Coorong, whose long narrow la-

ABOVE The ramparts of Mount Remarkable National Park. OPPOSITE Autumnal tones at Chateau Reynella winery.

goon and ramparts of dunes keep out the sea and follow the coast for 160 km (93 miles). The landscape is wild and desolate: the wind endlessly re-forms the dunes into new shapes and sea birds wheel in the spindrift. It is a national park which provides protection for the prodigious variety of wildlife and 150 species of birds and is a place of quiet and haunting beauty.

Robe, a historical gem 40 km (25 miles) beyond the Coorong, is now just a crayfishing port, a shadow of its former self of the 1860s. Then it was a major port that loaded cargoes of grain for England and landed hopeful Chinese bound for the gold diggings in Victoria.

The highway traverses a flat landscape scattered with lakes and reclaimed swamp for another 130 km (80 miles) before reaching **Mount Gambier**, third largest city in the State and set amidst the largest pine forest in Australia. Here you can join the daily tour to the timber mill just out of town and discover just what happens to the tree as it is processed into lumber. Mount Gambier enjoys a novel setting, built along the slopes of an extinct volcano whose lake in the crater floor holds the secret to one of nature's mysteries. Blue Lake abruptly changes color overnight every November, while two nearby lakes remain their original color. Nobody knows the reason for the change, but observation points are positioned around the crater rim to view the phenomenon.

HOTELS AND MOTELS

Hospitality Inn, Jubilee Highway, Mount Gambier. Tel: (087) 255122. 41 units. Rates: average.
Grandview Motel, 17 Lake Terrace West, Mount Gambier. Tel: (087) 3 255755. 35 units. Rates: average.

RIGHT The Flinders Ranges. OPPOSITE Wind has etched weird shapes into Remarkable Rocks on Kangaroo Island.

Macs Hotel, 21 Bay Road, Mount Gambier. Tel: (087) 252402. 14 rooms. Rates: budget.

HOW TO GET THERE

It takes almost six hours by bus and train from Adelaide to Mount Gambier.

HEADING NORTH

The coastal Princes Highway passes through green farmland which makes a pretty enough picture, but the inland route along road 32, which goes to Broken Hill, holds more fascination.

Admirers of Colonel Light's town-planning skills have dubbed **Gawler**, 40 km (25 miles) along the Sturt Highway, Athens of the North. The town does indeed retain a nineteenth-century charm and this has made it an attractive nearby alternative to living in Adelaide. Road 32 branches left off the highway soon

after leaving Gawler and it is another 40 km (25 miles) to **Kapunda**, Australia's first mining town following the discovery of copper. The entire town and mine area is listed by the Australian Heritage Council, and a museum in the former Baptist Church is worth browsing around for those who wish to recapture the atmosphere when South Australia was a fledgling colony. The mine was closed by flooding, but not before the town became the biggest in South Australia outside Adelaide and rich enough to ensure the survival of the State.

In **Burra**, another 87 km (54 miles) northward, stone cottages built 120 years ago for the copper miners remain today, unchanged as if time had stood still. Many miners and their families lived in earth dugouts, and two of these dugouts have been preserved in the dirt wall of a creek. The town has also kept its market place (where bare knuckle fights were staged), old pubs and jail.

A half-hour drive over the low hills brings you to the serene world of the Clare Valley. **Clare** is noted for its tree-lined streets – in fact one row of century-old oaks has the honor of comprising the only trees in the State listed by the National Trust.

The town is surrounded by a dozen vineyards; one which you can visit is operated by Jesuit brothers and produces most of Australia's altar wine – they even export it to overseas churches.

An hour's drive along peaceful back roads, lined with fields growing grain and paddocks dotted with cattle and sheep, brings you back on to the Princes Highway and to Port Pirie. Port Pirie is a modest industrial city with little more than a fancy Regency style railroad station to lift it from mediocrity.

Another hour up the road is **Port Augusta**, busy rail junction and crossroads, where it is possible to catch a direct train to Perth, Alice Springs, Sydney or Adelaide. Roads lead to the West, the Northern Territory and the eastern States for those with itchy feet

or the desire to delve deeper into the heart of Australia.

FLINDERS RANGES

Many visitors passing through Port Augusta are heading for the **Flinders Ranges**, whose peaks and ridges, many tens of millions of years old, cut a dramatic jagged path through South Australia.

Showpiece of the ranges is **Wilpena Pound**, an amphitheater whose rocky walls and cliffs encircle the bowl for 35

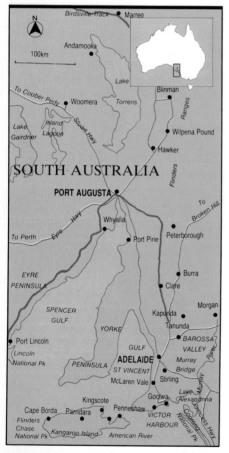

km (22 miles). The only way in is along a track through the sole gap in the ramparts. The bowl itself is covered in woodland and flowering bushes, and five walking trails snake across the floor. The earth is split by a number of

148

gorges and some of the dirt roads through the range wind through them.

The range is rich in Aboriginal carvings and lore, and experts date examples of the artistry as twenty thousand years old. Legend has it that Arkaroom the serpent created the range and formed the gorges by wriggling. He then slithered westward to Lake Frome and drank it dry, which is why there is never any water in the lake. He now sleeps in the Yacki water hole in the Gammon Ranges.

HOW TO GET THERE

It's about five hours by road from Adelaide, and there are also multi-day tours, some of them in four-wheel drive vehicles which take you into the most remote regions. Week-long backpacking treks are also available in Wilpena Pound and the Gammon Ranges, both national park areas.

OFF THE BEATEN TRACK

Port Augusta is the gateway to the formidable north, a harsh world of floating horizons, blinding salt lakes and little vegetation; a land where your nearest neighbor might be hundreds of kilometers away and you keep in touch with the rest of the world by radio. Two tracks strike out from Port Augusta across the wilderness, one into Queensland and the other into Central Australia.

BIRDSVILLE TRACK

To travel along the road to Queensland is one of the adventures of Australia, 486 km (303 miles) of bone shaking discomfort on the infamous Birdsville Track. Beginning at the township of **Maree**, in a parched area 397 km (250 miles) north of Port Augusta, the Track is one of Australia's best-known but least-traveled roads. Established as a route for cattle drives out of Queensland, the route has gained an image of intrepid romance; however, in reality it is dust and bumps and heat all the way. It crosses the sharp gibbers of Sturt's Stony Desert, always a hazard for vehicles, so be careful.

The best time to travel is from July to September as travelers at other times have been known to be stranded for days, and even weeks, after heavy rains have made the track impassible.

Even when you get to Birdsville, there is not much to greet you. It's an isolated one-pub hamlet still hundreds of kilometers away from a town of any size in Outback Queensland. But if you are heading for eastern Queensland and want to trim hundreds of kilometers from the journey, the Track is a shortcut.

HOW TO GET THERE

Check with the Government Travel Centre as some aspects of your journey could be affected by the weather and time of year.

OFF TO THE ALICE

The Stuart Highway into the Centre passes through hundreds of kilometers of desolation – dried-out claypans, saltbush and desert in which man lives and works for disparate reasons.

The road abruptly changes direction at Pimba 170 km (106 miles) out of Port Augusta in order to skirt the Woomera Prohibited Area; a 500 km (312 mile) expanse which in past years was a rocket range and site for British atomic tests. Woomera base itself is shrouded in secrecy and don't expect a red carpet; you are not even welcome and are only allowed in during daylight. Note that you are also not allowed to leave the highway where it crosses the restricted area.

Another 438 km (273 miles) ahead is

the world's largest opal- producing town, **Coober Pedy**, which is not all it seems. The fierce heat often exceeds 50°C (122°F), so a large number of the stoic miners have made their homes underground in abandoned workings. If you are lucky enough to be invited to have a look around one, you are in for a surprise. They have been dug out into spacious comfortable homes with a number of rooms, and fitted with carpets, electrical appliances and every convenience. Even the church is underground and so is the accommodation at

two of the five motels. No wonder the name means "White Man's Burrow" in the local Aboriginal dialect.

The surface of the town resembles an untidy moonscape, with dirt heaps from hundreds of abandoned and working mines. As well as the heat, there is also the dust to contend with and dust storms

TOP Advice for drivers in the arid outback.
LOWER A Coober Pedy miner washes for opals.

regularly blot out the surroundings. Only the most resolute tolerate the conditions for any length of time. Tours and demonstrations of opals being cut are laid on every day and you can buy stones or jewelry before setting out on the 732 km (455 mile) trek to Alice Springs.

HOW TO GET THERE

There are coach and air tours to Coober Pedy and a daily Adelaide-Alice bus service, a 26-hour trip. By road it is 12 hours from Adelaide to Coober Pedy.

MIGHTY MURRAY

The romantic days of the River Murray's great paddle wheelers have not disappeared altogether. The gold era lives on in a number of modern wheelers (now fitted with all mod cons – one even has a sauna) which cruise Australia's mightiest stream on trips lasting up to six days.

These nostalgic journeys are through waters where a century ago hundreds of paddleboats and barges went about their business. Today's cruise boats churn gently by quiet billabongs and settlements whose large wharves recall a more active past.

A trip up the river into the heartland of South Australia should begin at **Goolwa**, near its mouth. The river flows slowly in great sweeping bends between lush irrigated farmland, and 35 km (22 miles) upstream passes Murray Bridge, which began as a river crossing for cattle drives. **Mannum**, 30 km (19 miles) further inland, was the spot where river traffic began. The first steamer was built in the town in 1854 and its boiler is mounted on the riverbank as a monument to those days when boats steamed down

the main street during floods. The 80-year-old *Marion* is a maritime museum.

Waikerie marks the start of the Riverland, a 70 km (43 mile) long oasis, irrigated by the river, that each year yields two million tons of fruit, mountains of soft fruit and two out of every five bottles of Australian wine. The riverbank fertility is isolated, however, as the bushland takes over immediately you leave the orderly irrigated area. Waikerie also has a koala sanctuary and a reserve protecting precious mallee fowl.

Loxton is a neat riverside town of parks and trees, and another 25 km (15 miles) eastward is Berri, known across Australia as the brand name of the fruit juices manufactured here. Its winery is the largest in the Southern Hemisphere, with a storage capacity of 34 million liters (more than 40 million bottles).

Another two hours' gentle steaming away is **Renmark**, chief town of the Riverland. The National Trust has preserved the century- old log cabin home of the Chaffey brothers, Canadian-born brothers who pioneered irrigation in Australia and brought into being the Renmark scheme. Their home is open to the public.

HOW TO GET THERE

The *Murray River Queen* leaves Goolwa on five-day cruises, the *Murray Princess* operates out of Renmark into New South Wales on six-day cruises, and *Proud Mary* leaves from Murray Bridge. Houseboats are available for rent at several places.

ABOVE Many people in the remote opal mining town of Coober Pedy have carved out underground homes to avoid the heat. LEFT A tourist mine.

Western Australia

A New Frontier

PERTH

Perth stands sentinel 4,000 km (2,485 miles) from the cities of eastern Australia - Sydney is as far away from Perth as is Singapore. A city young at heart, it confidently sees Western Australia as the "new frontier" of the nation. And its residents are almost fiercely proud that they are out there all on their own.

The city is thoughtfully situated on a broad stretch of the River Swan of almost lake-like proportions, a location which imparts a feeling of spaciousness and brings the bonus of a sailing playground right on the doorstep - despite being 19 km (12 miles) upstream from the Indian Ocean. Heavy industry is conveniently located some distance to the south.

Perth even has its own natural thermostat, a breeze known as the Fremantle Doctor, which regularly wafts in from the ocean on hot summer afternoons and cools off the city and the beautiful beaches strung along the shore.

The business explosion which ac-

companied the opening up of huge iron ore deposits during the 1960s put the city into overdrive and transformed the skyline, but luckily sufficient public outcry and civic concern saved many historic buildings from the wreckers' hammer and the preserved heritage now harmonizes with new high-rise urban development.

ABOVE The Swan widens to almost lake-like proportions as it flows past Perth. OPPOSITE freeways snake through parkland into the city.

PERTH'S PAST

Fears of a French occupation of the western half of the continent spurred the establishment of Perth in 1819, all of 41 years after the setting up of the Sydney settlement. Expedition leader Captain James Stirling found the picturesque site he was looking for, and the people of Perth - now nudging a million - have been enjoying the wisdom of his choice ever since.

The colony began as a free settlement, but when growth slowed because of a labor shortage, it was necessary to bring in convict labor to boost the flagging economy.

The city grew very slowly, but the discovery of gold in 1890 at Coolgardie, and the opening of Fremantle harbor at the turn of the century, spurred rapid development.

Once again it was minerals which gave Perth the second great surge in its history. Staggeringly large amounts of iron ore were found in the Pilbara region 1,000 km (625 miles) to the north,

and Perth was the obvious choice for the headquarters of the Australian and international financiers and businessmen who arrived to set about mining the riches.

Tourist Information

The Holiday W.A. Centre is at 772 Hay Street, next to the Wesley Centre. Tel: (09) 322 2999. The staff can supply all the brochures you need and also make bookings.

TOURING PERTH

Pride and joy is **King's Park**, 404 hectares (1,000 acres) of gardens and bushland on the western edge of the central district. They provide a splendid viewpoint from which to look out over the busy streets and the Swan River. Explorer/politician John Forrest, who played a leading role in shaping the West, set the first area aside in 1872 for children "a thousand years hence to see what the bush was like when Stirling came here." Between August and November the park is a mass of beautiful

wildflowers, living examples of the wisdom of Forrest's foresight.

The park looks down across the Narrows Bridge to the colony's first flour mill, passed by speeding traffic on the Kwinana Freeway. The bridge's approach roads originally threatened to sweep away the 150-year-old landmark, until it was firmly suggested by the populace that authorities reconsider the idea. The free Green Clipper bus service takes you from the northeast corner of the park on the short ride back to Perth's main street, **St George's Terrace**.

Stroll along "The Terrace" and you pass a mixture of the city's oldest buildings and the glittering glass towers of the boom of the last two decades. At your feet are 150 bronze plaques which have been set into the sidewalk, each one honoring a Western Australian who made an outstanding contribution during the State's first 150 years.

Around the corner of Barrack Street from the eye-catching Treasury is Perth's **Town Hall**, built by convicts in the 1860s in the fashion of an English Jacobean market hall. It is said that the broad arrow-shape of the clock tower windows are a defiant gesture by the builders - it is however a common characteristic of this type of architecture.

Running along the southern side of the terrace is **Stirling Gardens**, part of the strip of parks, gardens and playing fields along the waterfront. The area set aside in the first year of settlement as botanic gardens is today the scene of concerts and art shows. The art gallery and museum, on the northern side of Horseshoe Bridge, incorporates Perth's original jail, built by luckless convicts for their own confinement. The shady, peaceful gardens are the scene of the hangings which occasionally took place - a grisly reminder of the city's past that comes as a shock

OPPOSITE The magnificent decorated dome of His Majesty's Theatre in Perth, a fitting showcase for ballet.

in such a picturesque setting.

SHOPPING

Shopping can be an adventure and don't be surprised if you get lost - but just ask a friendly face and you will be pointed in the right direction. City authorities blocked off part of **Hay Street** - buses being replaced by buyers, buskers and barrows - and a labyrinth of multi-level arcades have straggled off the pedestrian-only mall. Best known is **London Court**, a mock-Tudor alley of carved

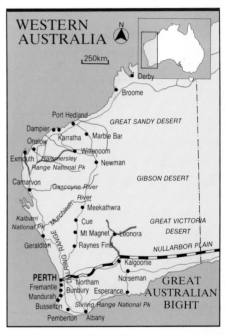

woodwork, lattice windows, wrought iron and dungeon towers.

There is a wide choice of Aboriginal art for sale, which make an exciting and different souvenir. **Aboriginal Art**, at 224 St George's Terrace, is a government-authorized outlet for authentic items, while **Dreamtime Gallery**, in the Merlin Centre, Plain Street, offers bark paintings by some of the most accomplished Arnhem Land painters. Modern works by prominent Aboriginal painters are at the **Gallery of Original Arts and Artifacts** in Croke Lane, Fremantle. Opals are a specialty in several shops, and at **Opal Exploration Company** in Hay Street mall you can watch gemstones being cut and polished.

HOW TO GET ABOUT

Clipper buses, free and color-coded, follow various inner routes. Ace, Ansett Pioneer, Feature and Parlorcars all operate half-day tours of the city sights, and all (except Ansett Pioneer) leave from the Holiday W.A. Centre in Hay Street. Scenic river cruises leave from Barrack Street jetty.

PERTH BY NIGHT

The international attention that was all part of winning the America's Cup in 1983 gave a boost to the nightlife here. Perth now boasts a $300 million casino complex which also incorporates a top-class hotel and 16,000-seat entertainment center.

Clubs are scattered around town and there is no single area of bright lights, but most clubs rave on until 3:30 am. **Hannibal's** in Northbridge is lively,

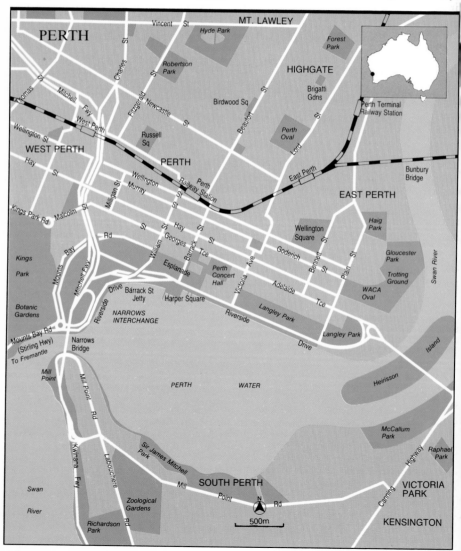

and **Jules** in Murray Street caters for the young crowd with a different type of music every night - funk one night, soul the next, etc. **Pinocchios** is also in Murray Street and has lots of room for jiving, while just along the street is the **Musos Club**, the place where musicians play for the rockers and for their own peers.

Crazy Cats, in William Street, specializes in a succession of shapely strippers, while in the same street is **River Cruise**, a singles nightclub which allows women in free of charge. The Old Melbourne Hotel in Hay Street features lingerie parades and strippers by day and comedians by night in its **Fitzroy's Club**; while upstairs **Mecannos** caters for those into alternative fashions and hairstyles. The **Red Lion Tavern** in Aberdeen Street, Northbridge, is a gathering place for gays. Lots of pubs feature bands, with the **Hyde Park Hotel** in Bulwer Street the headquarters of the Perth Jazz Society.

The Concert Hall in St George's Terrace features anything from grand opera to folk concerts, and there is also a concert hall and theater at the University of Western Australia campus at Nedlands. There are accomplished professional and amateur theater groups and their imaginative and innovative performances are worth looking out for.

The hundreds of restaurants embrace a smorgasbord of cuisines, so you shouldn't have too much trouble finding something to suit your taste.

Tours By Night

Ace, Feature and Parlorcars operate tours which include dinner, and there are also night cruises along the Swan on Fridays and Saturdays from Barrack Street jetty.

HOTELS AND MOTELS

Parmelia Hilton International, Mill Street. Tel: (09) 322 3622. 387 rooms and suites. Rates: expensive.

Ansett International, 10 Irwin Street. Tel: (09) 325 0481. 243 rooms and suites. Rates: expensive.

Mounts Bay Lodge, 116 Mounts Bay Road. Tel: (09) 321 8022. 67 units. Rates: average.

Greetings Wellington Street, 875 Wellington Street. Tel: (09) 322 6061. 79 rooms and suites. Rates: average.

Criterion Hotel, 560 Hay Street. Tel: (09) 325155. 61 rooms. Rates: average.

Southway Lodge, 35 Angelo Street, South Perth. Tel: (09) 367 5273. 20 suites. Rates: budget.

Beatty Park Motel, 235 Vincent Street, North Perth. Tel: (09) 328 1288. Rates: budget.

Jewell House, 180 Goderich Street. Tel: (09) 325 8488. 200 rooms. Rates: budget. This is a YMCA private hotel.

RESTAURANTS

Lady Ponsonby's, Piccadilly Square,

ABOVE View across the Swan from Royal Perth Yacht Club, the only club outside the United States to win the America's Cup.

East Perth. Game dishes in season are highly recommended.

Garden Restaurant, Parmelia Hilton. Elegant creative cuisine with the emphasis on fresh and seasonal dishes.

Bohemia, 309 William Street. Yugoslav/ Italian cuisine, with the best cevapcici in town. No frills, but top service.

HOW TO GET THERE

Perth is a terminus for one of the world's great train journeys, the transcontinental Indian-Pacific, which takes 64 hours between Perth and Sydney. Across the Nullarbor Plain it travels along the world's longest stretch of straight track - 482 km (300 miles). By comparison, the Perth-Adelaide Trans-Australian takes only 42 hours but is still a very pleasant and interesting journey.

Perth is an international air gateway, and a transit stop for flights traveling on to the east coast. Ansett and Australian Airlines services to Sydney and Melbourne take four hours.

Go west by road and you discover just how big Australia is - two and a half days to Sydney, 35 hours to Adelaide and almost 48 hours to Melbourne.

OUT OF PERTH

FREMANTLE

Fremantle, Perth's port 19 km (12 miles) downstream at the mouth of the Swan, was a humble work-a-day sea port where nothing much happened - until September 26 1983. That was the day that Australia won the America's Cup yachting trophy from the United States - and set off the wildest national celebrations since the end of World War II.

Fremantle suddenly found itself dragged out of its uneventful existence and into the center of a massive new building spree to prepare for the invasion in 1987 of the world's yachting

jet-setters who came to watch the Cup defense series. Today the tightly-woven and salty narrow streets are lined with a mixture of the old - the Round House dates back to 1831 and is the State's oldest building - and the new - blocks of accommodation, renovated hotels rejuvenated restaurants, sidewalk cafes ranks of marinas and compounds to house the sleek racing boats.

Walk down to the waterfront **Esplanade** and you can stand at the spot where Captain Fremantle of the British Navy landed in 1829, raised the Union Jack and "took possession of all that part of New Holland which is not included in the territory of New South Wales."

It is well worth making the effort while in Fremantle to visit the **Western Australia Maritime Museum,** where a most intriguing collection of seafaring history has been assembled during the past years and put on display. Marine architects are restoring the hull of the Dutch treasure ship *Batavia*, wrecked off the Western Australian coast near Geraldton, 330 km (206 miles) north of Perth, in 1629.

Divers recovered the timbers, which they numbered on the seabed, and museum experts began a delicate preserving process lasting several years. The waterlogged timbers were placed in vats of wax, which gradually replaces the water and prevents the wood from collapsing. This method has already been successfully used to preserve a Viking long boat.

Tourist Information

Fremantle council runs an office facing St John's Square, tel: (09) 335 2952.

HOW TO GET THERE

Catch a bus from Wellington Street or a cruise launch from No. 2 jetty.

OPPOSITE Fremantle's Round House, originally a jail and the West's oldest (1831) building.

ROTTNEST ISLAND

One of Perth's favorite getaway destinations, the island 19 km (12 miles) offshore possesses a shoreline of picturesque bays and long beaches. Its most famous inhabitants are the quokkas, small wallaby-like marsupials. A Dutch explorer who landed in the seventeenth century mistook them for rats and called the place Rats' Nest - a name which has stuck.

Surrounding reefs protect the island and make its waters excellent for swimming - in fact skin-diving enthusiasts can look at some of the most southerly coral in the world. There is a hotel and other reasonably-priced accommodation if you wish to stay the night. A bus tours the flat island and you can also hire a bicycle and do your own exploring. However cars, along with pets and spearguns, are banned.

HOW TO GET THERE

Ferries leave Barrack Street jetty at 9 am daily, and the trip takes between one and two hours, depending on which vessel you choose. There is also a 15-minute flight from Perth airport.

THE HINTERLAND

An arc of scenic and interesting countryside runs in a broad sweep to the east of Perth.

The road out through Guildford heading northeast passes through the neatly-patterned vineyards of the Swan Valley. The first vines were planted soon after the first settlers landed, and today's wineries make wines that are generally more fruity than those of the eastern States.

The main national park on the fringe of the city, **John Forrest National Park**, is only a few minutes' drive to the east of the Swan Valley. Here Rocky streams and waterfalls tumble through beautiful bushland settings that make ideal picnic spots.

The **Darling Range**, which sweeps southward from the park for another 350 km (220 miles), is an area of winding roads and tracks that meander through the low hills and make for a leisurely afternoon's drive.

Mandurah a few kilometers south of Perth is ideal for family holidays and

many people from Perth go no further. The resort is at the mouth of a network of inland waterways with 150 km (93 miles) of shoreline and 40 km (25 miles) of magnificent beaches. Amateur fishermen flock to the rivers and inlets, and the coast is ideal for sailing and surfing.

HOW TO GET THERE

Cruise companies operate launches up the Swan Valley, and one of the coach tours out of Perth includes a cruise

along the Mandurah waterways. All major coach companies run a variety of day excursions to take in the vineyards, Darling Range and the Mandurah coast.

WHERE OCEANS MEET

The extreme southwest corner of the continent, where the polar rollers of the Southern Ocean pound one coastline and the Indian Ocean rolls in on the western seaboard, is the only lush part of Western Australia - thanks to the generous prevailing rain-bearing winds. Forests of giant trees, narrow roads passing through enchanting countryside, limestone caves eroded by time, are all found here.

Bunbury, three hours south of Perth by train and the State's first provincial town to be given city status, is a convenient starting place.

A few kilometers to the north is the village of Australind, where services are still held in Australia's smallest church. St Nicholas', a converted cottage built in the 1840s, is 8.2 m (27 ft) long and 3.6 m (12 ft) wide. A novel way of seeing the countryside around Bunbury is by steam train behind two quaint locomotives from the past - Leschenault Lady and Koombana Queen. They regularly ply a fascinating little line which follows a pretty route through the Darling Range. The Bunbury information office, in Arthur Street, tel: (097) 214737, will give you train times.

The road south leads to the Margaret River area, the axe-head shaped tip of land which sticks out into the ocean. **Busselton** is a resort of sweeping beaches and a favorite getaway destination from Perth during summer holidays, while Margaret River itself is the center of the region's newest industry - wine. Ten minutes' drive from Busselton is the hamlet of Prevelly Park, named by a former resident in tribute to the monks of Preveli monastery in Crete, who sheltered him and other escaped prisoners during World War II. A Greek Orthodox Church on the hillside is dedicated to all Cretans.

TIMBER COUNTRY

The Brockman Highway heads eastward and is soon dappled in shade, for this is the country of the tall timbers, home of the majestic karri trees which are found nowhere else in Australia. The hardwood giants tower more than 75 m (240 ft) and form a canopy over a 150 km (95 miles) sweep of countryside under which is a hushed world of shadows and bird calls. The tallest tree felled was of a height equivalent to a 35-story building, and at the timber town of **Pemberton** you can climb up to the 64 m (210 ft) lookout - Gloucester Tree - but only at your own risk.

A further 240 km (150 miles) southward along the South Western Highway lies **Albany**, the first settlement in the West (although Perth was to come three years later to take both the power and the glory). The town boasts more "oldest" records than any other place in Western Australia. It has the oldest consecrated church, the oldest post office, and the oldest house, Strawberry Hill, which was once the home of the government representative, and is open daily. On the waterfront is a replica of the brigantine *Amity*, the vessel which in 1826 brought a small party of soldiers and convicts from Sydney to lay claim to the West.

Stirling Range National Park, 60 km (37 miles) north of Albany, ranks as one of Australia's most outstanding botanical reserves. It is an area of jagged slopes that rise with dramatic suddenness from the surrounding plain making them appear larger than they are. The range is covered by hundreds of species of plants, some of which are found nowhere else in the world. The most rare may be found in only a small area, so it is worth doing a little research first. Bush walkers rate the tracks among the most attractive to be found and a stroll through the area is highly recommended.

From the park it's about five hours by road back to Perth, through the fringe of the wheat belt.

OPPOSITE The tall timbers of the south-west, and the blue-misted walls of the Stirling Range.

HOTELS AND MOTELS

Dog Rock Motel, 303 Middleton Road, Albany. Tel: (098) 414422. 80 units. Rates: average.
Ace Motel, 314 Albany Highway, Albany. Tel: (098) 412911. 55 units. Rates: average.
Valencia Lodge, 4 Valencia Close, Albany. Tel: (098) 416741. Rates: budget.

HOW TO GET THERE

Westrail lays on a number of tours out

of Perth, from a day in Bunbury to a comprehensive 6-day exploration of the southwest. The Australind train leaves Perth at 9:30 am every morning except Sunday for Bunbury, and Westrail also provides a bus service. The Westrail bus to Albany takes up to six and a half hours from Perth, depending on day and route. Skywest flies to Bunbury and Albany on weekdays.

WILDFLOWERS

Western Australia also likes to call itself the Wildflower State, and this is as good an opportunity as any to mention the West's unique floral magnificence.

Shielded from the remainder of the continent by a barrier of deserts, and isolated from the rest of the world by ocean, Western Australia has become a vast insulated garden in which thousands of varieties of wildflowers have been able to develop undisturbed through many millenniums. From late winter until summer, visitors from all over Australia and biological experts from overseas come to see the most colorful natural display in Australia. The predominant colors are yellows and blues, though it is a virtual patchwork quilt that delights the eye.

About half of the varieties on the continent are in the West, and about three quarters of these are to be found in the moist southwest corner, while others have adapted to the desert. About seven thousand flowering species, with the Proteaceae family of grevilleas and banksias accounting for more than five hundred of these, make up the total. Some orchids even live and flower underground in a unique adaptation to a harsh environment.

How to See Them

Wildflower tours originate in all States. Contact the Holiday W. A. Centre in Perth or W. A. Travel Centres in other cities for information on the best months and places to see the flowers. If you are short of time, many of the flowers can be seen in King's Park in Perth.

THE GOLDEN MILE

Kalgoorlie is often the name that comes to mind when thinking of Australian gold rushes.

The fabulous strike of the 1890s brought prospectors flocking, and the dry scrub semi-desert quickly spawned an ant-hill of tents, shacks and mine shafts. Thousands of fortunes were made - and more than a few lost or squandered away - as the cluster of mines between Kalgoorlie and the twin town of Boulder became known as the Golden Mile, the richest square mile on earth.

Those heady days of high hopes and big dreams are long gone, but gold is still being mined and the town has clung to its

OPPOSITE A bob-tailed lizard in a desert national park. ABOVE Kalgoorlie's Golden Mile.

rough-and-ready image with its buildings sporting wooden verandahs and wrought iron balconies. The **Palace**, best-known of the hotels, still exudes an Edwardian atmosphere; while Western Australia's only legal two-up school outside Perth (the traditional, and usually illegal, gambling game played with two coins) flourishes in the bush a few kilometers out of the town and is even on coach-tour visiting lists. The Hainault tourist mine, on the **Golden Mile**, takes visitors 304 m (1,000 ft) underground to show them

even the richest Victoria field, it yielded more than 31 million ounces of gold.

In its heyday the town had two stock exchanges and six newspapers. Today relics and mining rubbish dot the countryside and one hundred and fifty markers, illustrated with old photographs, show how the town once looked. **The Goldfields Exhibition** in the Warden's Court Building is the most comprehensive prospecting museum in the State, and there is also a railway museum for those who like the romance of the old trains.

how the mine once worked.

Ghosts are more plentiful than gold these days in the surrounding bush, where other gold mines once thrived. A few townships have disappeared entirely, others such as Broad Arrow, Gwalia and Ora Banda survive as desolated ruins and are only inhabited by a handful of people who feel no urge to move.

Most famous of the ghost towns is **Coolgardie**, whose field produced the bonanza to top them all. Richer than

The strikes in the Kalgoorlie-Coolgardie fields set off the last full-blooded gold rush in Australia and brought to an end four remarkable decades of the nation's history.

Goldfield Tours
Goldfield Tours operate half-day tours of Kalgoorlie and the ghost towns.

HOTELS AND MOTELS

Hospitality Inn, Hannan Street, Kal-

goorlie. Tel: (090) 212888. 54 rooms.
Rates: average.
Palace Hotel, Hannan Street. Tel:
(090) 212788. 47 rooms. Rates: average.
Railway Hotel, corner Wilson and Forrest streets. Tel: (090) 213047. Rates: budget.

HOW TO GET THERE

The Prospector leaves Perth station daily except Saturday, and takes seven and a half hours for the 600 km (375

mile) journey. Coach and air services operate daily, and most tours of the area last two days.

THE LONG ROUTE NORTH

It is only when you begin to travel outside the populated southwest that you realize just how vast Western Australia is.

Texans boast that their State is large; Western Australia is three and a half times as big. You can take off in a jet aircraft in one corner, and four hours later still be flying over Western Australia. It is 4,000 km (2,485 miles) by road from the southwest corner to the Northern Territory border and you cross from one climatic zone to another along the way. The uninhabited and almost rainless Centre is three deserts merged into one, a harsh and empty wasteland with some of the oldest land formations on earth.

Daunting distances make a round-trip to the north impractical unless you have ample time, so the most sensible alternative is a one-way trip between Perth and the Northern Territory along the main road, the North West Coastal Highway. Buses and aircraft service the coastal towns daily, and extended coach tours operate out of Perth. There is no railroad.

The highway passes through the edge of the West's huge wheat belt - Western Australia is the biggest wheat-growing State after New South Wales - on its way to **Geraldton**, one of only five towns of consequence on the road to the Territory. A five-hour drive from Perth, Geraldton is the home port of Western Australia's largest crayfishing fleet, whose multi-million dollar catch is exported to the United States and Europe.

In **Geraldton Museum** are relics from many of the Dutch treasure ships wrecked off the coast in the seventeenth and eighteenth centuries while on their way to Java. Some of the relics are from the remains of the *Batavia*, which in 1629 was the scene of the first act of infamy by the white man in Australia. The crew mutinied after the ship struck a reef on islands offshore, and they massacred one hundred and twenty five men, women and children in a plan to seize the cargo of silver. Justice pre-

OPPOSITE Reflections of Kalgoorlie's historic main street. ABOVE The Pinnacles in Tambung National Park.

vailed, however, and the murderers were hanged.

Hutt River Province is an hour north of Geraldton, but you won't find it on any official maps as the government chooses not to acknowledge it. The province is ruled by Prince Leonard, otherwise Leonard Casley, a farmer who formed his breakaway State after a row with authorities about the amount of wheat he was allowed to grow. His 7,470 hectare (18,500 acre) principality has its own passports, stamps and money, which are not recognized by any government but are fun for their novelty value.

Kalbarri National Park, just west of the highway from Hutt, is an area of spectacular gorges, twisting and looping between towering rock walls, sheer coastal cliffs and more than five hundred species of wildflowers. Roads conveniently go to all the best lookouts from where you can fully appreciate the park's breath-taking grandeur.

The flat coastal highway unfolds for another 400 km (250 miles) to **Carnarvon,** a large fishing and farming town which is now a rapidly expanding producer of fruit and vegetables, grown with the help of irrigation schemes.

On and on the road stretches ahead, around the northwestern shoulder of the continent for almost 1,000 km (620 miles) to the ports and towns of the Pilbara, where iron ore arrives from the massive mines hundreds of kilometers back in the harsh and dry Outback. The Pilbara represents the most staggering explosion of industry Australia has known, and in just two decades iron ore has become the mainstay of the Australian West's economy. Tens of thousands of people lured by high salaries live in the orderly, air-conditioned company towns such as Tom Price, Newman and Goldsworthy and endure this hot and isolated region.

Visitors are able to tour the loading facilities at the deepwater ports of **Dampier** and **Port Hedland,** where the ore is loaded for shipment to Japanese and other Asian steel mills. They can stay in four-star hotel comfort at **Karratha,** a satellite town being developed near Dampier, in the Karratha International: the only four-star hotel in the State outside Perth.

The thousands of trees which give the company towns welcome shade and greenery have all been shipped hundreds of kilometers to make the lives of miners and their families that touch more pleasant.

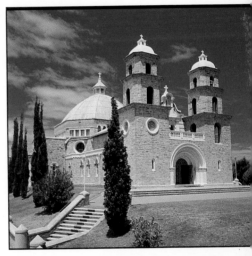

By the time you arrive at Broome on the remote West Kimberley coast, you are 2,253 km (1,400 miles) north of Perth and 500 km (310 miles) beyond the Pilbara.

Once the boisterous capital of the north, the faded and picturesque town now has more the atmosphere of the South Pacific; a mood enhanced by the polyglot population of the descendants of Japanese, Malay, Chinese, Arab and European pearlers. Chinatown, once the haunt of tough lugger crews, is now the main shopping area with trading stores, a Japanese shrine and the old divers' quarters. Several companies grow cul-

OPPOSITE Sand patterns at Eucla. ABOVE The Byzantine-style St Francis Xavier Cathedral at Geraldton.

tured pearls, and you can watch them being sorted into size and color.

Travel for another two and a quarter hours and you are at Derby, the cattle shipping outlet for the huge properties of the Kimberley, also famous for its grotesque boab trees with their weird bottle-shaped trunks. Aborigines of the Mowanjum community carve ancient and intricate designs on boab nuts, which they sell as souvenirs. The cattle ranches stretch for huge distances and were founded a century ago by doughty cattlemen and their families after the longest drives the world has ever known. Herds were driven from Queensland and New South Wales on treks which sometimes lasted more than three years.

In its remaining 900 km (560 miles) to the Territory border, the highway passes through empty scorched country, with only the tiny cow town of Fitzroy Crossing and Hall's Creek to break the tedium.

Kununurra, a half-hour drive from the border, is a tidily laid-out township born in the 1960s and hub of the ambitious Ord River Scheme. This $100 million project was to dam the river and the waters are now being used in a vast irrigation system. Don't miss a visit to Argyle Downs homestead, home of the pioneering Durack family, who in a two-year trek drove two thousand head of cattle from Queensland and founded an empire. The house was originally some distance away, only to be dismantled and re-erected on its present site to save it being drowned by the irrigation scheme's Lake Argyle.

HOW TO GET THERE

Greyhound, Ansett Pioneer and Deluxe all operate Perth-Darwin services, the trip taking two and a half days. Traveling times from Perth are six hours to Geraldton, 12 hours to Carnarvon, 24 hours to Port Hedland, 31 hours to Broome, 37 hours to Derby and 49 hours to Kununurra. Ansett and TAA also fly the route daily. Coach tours by necessity include the highway on extended and round-Australia tours.

OFF THE BEATEN TRACK

The back road to the north, the Northern Highway, is a hot, dry short-cut through unforgiving Outback wilderness skirting the great deserts of the inland. The road from Perth is sealed for only half its distance of 1,335 km (830 miles) before it joins the coastal highway near Port Hedland.

The road follows the trail taken by goldminers heading south when the Kimberley lodes ran out, and a succession of almost-forgotten towns snooze lazily in the hot sun along its route.

Paynes Find, Cue, Mount Magnet and **Meekatharra** are all rundown hamlets littered with mining relics from better days (although Mount Magnet is back in business again because of rising gold prices), and you can even try for your own gold using a metal detector in an area set aside for amateur prospectors.

Traveling through this desolate scrubby landscape you suddenly see the welcome sight of humanity and greenery – the iron ore mining company town of **Newman,** where 60,000 trees soften the harshness. About 430 km (270 miles) north of Meekatharra, Newman houses miners working the biggest of the Pilbara's mines and the world's largest open-pit iron ore mine at **Mt Whaleback.** Guides will take you around an operation which is huge in every way, befitting an operation whose reserves are estimated at 1,400 million tons.

Last stop on the highway before it joins the coast road is **Marble Bar,** an historic gold township renowned as

Weathering in the outback. TOP LEFT Kalbarri National Park. TOP RIGHT and BOTTOM, The Pilbara.

Australia's hot-spot, which has an annual maximum temperature of 37.5°C (99°F); though it once topped 37.7°C (100°F) for 160 days in a row. Mining continues in a small way.

HOW TO GET THERE

Greyhound runs a bus each way three times a week, the trip taking 22-1/2 hours. Coach tours and safari tours also cover parts of the route. Inquire at the Holiday W.A. Centre in Perth for details.

THE GORGES

The Pilbara and the Kimberley regions consist of land forms going back 3,500 million years. Broad steep-sided canyons dramatic in their dimensions and grandeur have been gouged red and raw by the elements.

In the Hammersley Range National Park in the Pilbara, millions of years of rain has carved out the 45 km (27 mile) **Dale's Gorge.** This joins the **Red, Weano** and **Hancock Gorges** to meet at Oxer's Lookout. In contrast to the dry landscape the floors of the gorges are shaded by trees and speckled with cool pools – irresistibly inviting after a long trek across the wilderness.

The Kimberley Gorges are equally spectacular. **Geikie Gorge,** near Fitzroy Crossing, is awe-inspiring with the color of its walls constantly changing between golden and deepest red, according to the position of the sun. The gorge's origins go back 350 million years to when it was part of a coral reef which surfaced when the ocean level fell. Stingray and swordfish have adapted over generations to the fresh water and can still be observed by the patient visitor. Remarkable Aboriginal paintings decorate some cliff caves and are well worth taking a look at. **Windjana Gorge,** 100 km (65 miles) to the northwest, is a place that has been sacred to Aborigines for centuries.

HOW TO GET THERE

Anset Pioneer is one of the coach companies running a Gorges tour, and several safari tours also make the trip. Nor-West Explorer Tours of Karratha operate a three-day tour of the Hammersley Range gorges twice a week. Best time to travel in the north is between May and September.

Gorge country. CLOCKWISE FROM TOP LEFT Red Bluff, old mine in Wittenoom Gorge, Geikie Gorge National Park, Windjana Gorge, Dales Gorge in Hamersley Range National Park.).

Tasmania

The Past Lives On

HOBART

Of all the State capitals, Hobart is the one most successful in retaining its sense of history and nineteenth-century heritage.

Established only 16 years after Sydney and therefore Australia's second oldest city; the island's cosy little capital is endowed with some splendid buildings – and their Georgian elegance can almost make you forget that in many cases they were paid for with the toil of convicts.

Commercial pressures and growth have been more measured here – even today the population is only 160,000 – and there is a tranquil and easy-going and friendly atmosphere.

With the low profile of its buildings and a climate which at its best is warm but is often brisk in summer and decidedly chilly in winter; it has more of the imprint of Europe than contemporary mainland Australia.

No matter which way you turn there are constant reminders of Hobart's majestic setting, which for sheer beauty vies with that of Sydney. The brooding backdrop is Mt Wellington, its summit often hidden in cloud or dusted with snow; while its front window is the broad estuary of the River Derwent, with views across the waters to rolling green farmlands and small suburbs.

The salty jauntiness of its port is only a stone's throw from shops and offices. Wharves, once lined with ocean-scarred whalers manned by brawling crews, now provide a haven for fishing vessels.

THE PAST

Hobart was established in 1804 as a penal colony to forestall any French intentions of possession. Like other Australian colonies it began with stumbling steps. The first settlement was further upriver, but this proved unsatisfactory and the move was made to Sullivan's Cove.

When Governor Macquarie came down from Sydney eight years later, he still found the place "without any plan whatever" and drew up the design for the main square and seven streets which now form the city center.

Various motions in early years to move the seat of government were defeated, and this brought the stability necessary to allow the orderly development of a town which was already a vital shipping center and to give it stature and dignity.

Tourist Information

The Tasbureau office, at 80 Elizabeth Street, tel: (002) 346911, will handle all your tour bookings and answer any queries. Ask for *Travelways*, the newspaper for visitors, and relevant "Let's Talk About..." brochures.

AROUND HOBART

Hobart is small enough to walk around. Most visitors make first for the waterfront and **Constitution Dock,** where you can see fresh fish being sold from the boats. This is the scene of noisy celebrations at the end of the year when crowds wait all through the night for finishers in the Sydney-Hobart yacht race, one of the world's most prestigious sailing events.

Walk south along Franklin Wharf past the cargo boats and river- cruise launches, and straight ahead are the graceful lines of **Parliament House** which was built by convicts in the 1830s as a Customs House (although many alterations and additions have since been made). When Parliament is in session visitors can view proceedings from the gallery, while on non-sitting days if you are fortunate, an attendant will show you around.

Follow the waterfront around the cove to **Salamanca Place,** which many claim to be the finest row of early warehouses in Australia. Financed from the wealth of the whaling trade in earlier days, the warehouses have been gracefully restored to house restaurants and art and craft galleries. On Saturday mornings the Place is abuzz with a colorful market and is packed with locals and tourists alike.

On higher ground behind the warehouses is **Battery Point,** a complete colonial-era village looking much as it did more than a century ago. The enclave of narrow jumbled streets retains military establishment dating from before the battle of Waterloo and still used by the army. You can wander around any day, and there are tours on Tuesday mornings.

On the other side of town, near the Tasman Bridge which you cross coming in from the airport, the Botanic Gardens are laid out with quiet walks, flowerbeds and cool ponds.

Upstream on the Derwent's eastern bank is Risdon Cove, the site of Hobart's first settlement. Archeologists have determined details of several structures

the maritime character of those times, when it was inhabited by captains and sailors, merchants and fishermen. One or two cottages have even been turned into bed-and-breakfast establishments, so it's worth seeking them out if you want to feel close to the heart of Hobart's history. The **Tasmanian Maritime Museum** is in Cromwell Street, and the **Van Diemen's Land Memorial Folk Museum** can be found in Hampden Street. Backing on to Hampden Street is **Anglesea Barracks,** Australia's oldest erected by the first party of convicts and soldiers. Two buildings house a display that provides a sobering reminder of the State's beginnings.

Mt Wellington, rearing 1,270 m (4,165 ft) behind the city, is as much a part of Hobart as the bricks and mortar of the buildings. From the top it is possible to see much of the southeast corner of the State. Choose your weather,

ABOVE The nursery rhyme place name animated with musical clock is an attraction at a Hobart shopping arcade.

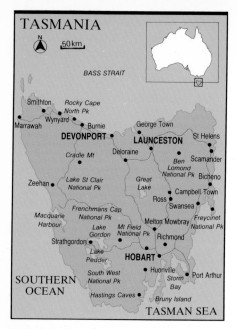

TASMANIA

N

50 km

BASS STRAIT

Smithton
Rocky Cape
North Pk
Wynyard
Marrawah
Burnie
George Town
DEVONPORT
LAUNCESTON
St Helens
Cradle Mt
Deloraine
Ben Lomond National Pk
Scamander
Bicheno
Zeehan
Lake St Clair National Pk
Great Lake
Campbell Town
Ross
Swansea
Frenchmans Cap National Pk
Macquarie Harbour
Melton Mowbray
Freycinet National Pk
Lake Gordon
Mt Field National Pk
Richmond
Strathgordon
Lake Pedder
HOBART
SOUTHERN OCEAN
South West National Pk
Huonville
Storm Bay
Port Arthur
Hastings Caves
Bruny Island
TASMAN SEA

however, as the peak is liable at any time of year to be wreathed in cloud. An imaginative tour operator recently launched a novel descent – by hire bicycle – which is fun but definitely not for the faint-hearted.

ARTS AND CRAFTS

Woodwork, leatherwork, basketry, pottery and homespun wool are the main craft items found in Hobart. Craft- and gift-shops also sell lightwood items made from the remarkable huon pine, an almost indestructible tree which grows only in the remote regions of the southwest. Its oil content ensures resistance to rot, and it retains its distinctive smell for decades. In the antique shops scattered around the city it is possible to find relics from convict days. The Crafts Council of Tasmania, in Salamanca Place, tel: (002) 235622, has compiled a directory.

OPPOSITE Hobart and wintery Mt Wellington. Tasman Bridge is one of 5,000 road bridges on the island, an average of a bridge every two and a half miles of road.

How to Get Around

Although you can visit most of Hobart's sights on foot, some places are too far away to walk to. Check with Tasbureau for bus services. Half-day coach tours explore the city, Mt Wellington and Risdon Cove, while several charter companies operate a variety of Derwent cruises from the south end of Sullivan's Cove.

HOBART BY NIGHT

Hobart has a commendably lively nightlife for such a small place. The brightest lights shine at **Wrest Point Casino** on Sandy Bay, a five-minute taxi ride from the city. International stars appear in cabaret and there is a stylish revolving restaurant with views over the city and river. The gaming rooms offer all the usual gambling variations for those keen to try their luck.

The Living Room's Disco, and **Beaujangles,** both in Victoria Street, are among the livelier nightspots, and there is jazz, folk and blues six nights a week at the noisy and packed **Dog House Hotel** on the corner of Barrack and Goulburn Streets.

HOTELS AND MOTELS

Innkeepers Lenna, 20 Runnymede Street, Battery Point. Tel: (002) 232911. 55 rooms and suites. Rates: expensive.
Wrest Point, 410 Sandy Bay Road. Tel: (002) 250112. 294 rooms and suites. Rates: expensive.
Hadley's Hotel, 34 Murray Street. Tel: (002) 234355. 90 rooms. Rates: average.
Prince of Wales Hotel, 55 Hampden Road, Battery Point. Tel: (002) 236355. Rates: average.
Globe Hotel, 178 Davey Street. Tel: (002) 235800. 12 rooms. Rates: budget.
Shamrock Hotel, 195 Liverpool Street. Tel: (002) 343892. 8 rooms. Rates: budget.

RESTAURANTS

Mure's Fish House, 5 Knopwood Street, Battery Point. Considered by some the best place in town for seafood. Book first.

Sisco's, 121 Macquarie Street. The emphasis here is on Spanish food, and the stuffed squid is recommended.

Prospect House, Richmond (20 minutes from town). Superb cooking, specializes in game.

HOW TO GET THERE

Hobart is served by two international air services, from Auckland and Christchurch in New Zealand. The only direct Ansett and Australian Airlines flights are from Melbourne and Sydney, passengers from other departure points have to transfer at either of these cities. East West Airlines also flies direct from Sydney and is cheaper, but less frequent.

THE PICTUREBOOK STATE

Within minutes of arriving in Tasmania you realize that this triangular appendage which looks as if it has slipped off the bottom of the continent is very different from mainland Australia. It has none of the heat, no shimmering horizons or blue dome skies. If the color associated with the mainland is red, then Tasmania is the green of a lush and well-watered land. With its temperate climate and narrow lanes winding between hedges of briar and hawthorn it is often likened to rural England. It is also a mountainous island, with large wilderness areas where man has not yet left his mark. Almost half is covered with forest, which makes it an ideal place for backpackers and hikers.

The other main difference between Tasmania and the rest of Australia is that there are no endless distances to be travelled before you feel you have arrived somewhere. From the south to the north is only a half-day drive and it's little more than two hours between Hobart and Launceston, the second city. Extended coach tours are between eight and fourteen days, ample time to see most of the State. Because of the compactness, many visitors choose to have

independent transport, either bringing their vehicles across the Bass Strait from Melbourne on the ferry, or hiring cars, and more especially mobile homes, once they get here. So grab some wheels and let's go exploring.

PORT ARTHUR

The spot which attracts most visitors is also the one with the blackest history - **Port Arthur**, the convict settlement 102 km (63 miles) southeast of Hobart on

the tip of the Tasman Peninsula.

The sinister shadow of Australia's convict past is more apparent in Tasmania than anywhere else, and while Port Arthur has the best preserved historical ruins, it is also the grimmest reminder of that sorry era. Between 1830 and the 1850s (Tasmania was still accepting convicts long after Sydney had ceased to) about 12,500 convicts, among them the most blackhearted, passed through its cells.

Some buildings have survived in better shape, such as the roofless church, the four-story penitentiary, the commandant's house, and the model prison, in which convicts who did not respond to discipline were confined in soundproof and totally dark cells until they mended their ways.

Across the bay lies Point Puer, where juvenile offenders were incarcerated; and off the point is the Isle of Dead, where 1,800 convicts are buried.

Despite its ghosts, Port Arthur is today a place of tranquillity and mellow stone buildings set among lawns and groves of English trees. The asylum has been turned into a visitors' center and museum that makes an ideal orientation point.

HOW TO GET THERE

Coach tours leave Hobart daily except Tuesday and Thursday. There is also a car tour, minimum four passengers. Check with Tasbureau for details.

HUON VALLEY

Before soaring freight prices and changing tastes soured the industry, Tasmania was known as The Apple Isle, with millions of cases each year exported to Europe and other overseas markets.

Today there are only 300 growers, most of them in the picturesque **Huon Valley**, south of Hobart, where orchards line the roadsides and march up the hillsides. The prettiest time is in October when the trees are in blossom. The Huon River opens out into a wide estuary, with villages such as Huonville, Geeveston and Dover lying quiety along its banks.

An alternative route back to Hobart follows the shoreline of the D'Entrecasteaux Peninsula, a coast of placid little bays and tree-covered headlands. Offshore lies **Bruny Island**, which can be reached by a car ferry from the village of Kettering. The French names on the map serve as gentle reminders that the English were not the only explorers to come this way.

HOW TO GET THERE

Coach tours do not operate every day so check with Tasbureau. Car tours operate as needed, but remember it's about a 200 km (125 mile) round trip.

SOUTHWEST WILDERNESS

The entire southwest corner is a land of stark mountain ranges, wild rivers, and swirling mists. The savage and remote region has an aura of grandeur and solitude. As one of the last remaining temperate wildernesses it has World Heritage List status.

The only way in is along the road to the village of Strathgordon. Turn off at New Norfolk, on the Lyell Highway 40 km (25 miles) north of Hobart, and then drive another 122 km (76 miles).

Strathgordon was built in the 1970s to house workers building a hydroelectric system, a project which sparked the most bitter conservation conflict seen in Australia since World War II. The scheme entailed flooding Lake Pedder, destroying rare plants and, according to critics, irreparably damaging the environment.

The all-powerful Hydro-Electric Commission won the battle and the access road now enables tens of thousands of tourists a year to enjoy the beauty of an area which previously had been closed to all but the hardiest backpackers.

Several places are worth a stop along the Strathgordon road. **New Norfolk** is among Tasmania's most picturesque old towns, with an inn claimed to be the oldest in the nation and a host of other historic buildings, including the State's oldest church which faces peacefully across a village green. An oasthouse, serving as a museum of the hop industry, is centered at **Bushy Park** 10 km (6 miles) along the road. The rows of hops which encircle the pretty village provide more than half of Australia's brewing needs and the scene is particularly beautiful in autumn when the rows of protective poplars turn to gold.

A few kilometers beyond Bushy Park is the entrance to Mt Field National Park, best known for **Russell Falls**, a glistening curtain of water - and only a short walk from the car park.

HOW TO GET THERE

A half-day coach tour to New Norfolk operates on Monday afternoons, and day-tours to Lake Pedder and Russell Falls on Tuesday and Saturdays.

OPPOSITE Russell Falls, one of several cascades in Mount Field National Park, ABOVE The guard tower at Port Arthur, the best preserved reminder of Australia's convict past.

Three roads connect north and south Tasmania - scenic, leisurely routes along the east and west coasts, with the faster and more practical Midland Highway arrowing through the central farmlands between Hobart and Launceston.

The western route, the most popular with visitors, climbs towards the central plateau with its mountains and windswept moors, tracing the source of the Derwent.

Derwent Bridge, a pub and little else 173 km (108 miles) from Hobart, is the turn-off for **Cradle Mountain National Park**, a rugged 1,270 sq km (490 sq mile) reserve of spectacular alpine scenery.

The view 80 km (50 miles) further on is of bare, stained hillsides among ravaged surroundings as you begin the steep drop down. The road twists and turns a hundred times into the historic mining town of **Queenstown**. The trees were felled to fuel the town's copper smelter, which in turn produced the fumes which killed the remaining vegetation and stained the countryside. In those days there were 11,000 people living here, and the town was a fabulously rich copper, gold and silver mining center whose wealth sustained Tasmania's economy for several decades. Now fewer than 4,000 residents remain, the good times are long gone and the future looks bleak. The town is now known only for its moonscape setting.

Strahan, another 40 km (25 miles) towards the coast, stands on the shore of Macquarie Harbour, whose islands include the infamous Settlement Island, the absolute end of the line for convicts beyond redemption. Prisoners were sent to this bleak rocky hump to labor in the shipyard and die in appalling conditions or at the hands of their fellow prisoners. Half-day tours operate out of Strahan.

The road winds through dramatic mountain scenery for another 180 km (112 miles) before reaching the coast at Somerset, a small resort.

The coast-hugging Bass Highway turns eastward and it is only a few kilometers to **Burnie**, the major port on the island's north coast. There is an imaginative **Pioneer Village Museum** in High Street. The highway runs through fertile farmland and small resorts to **Devonport**, the gateway to Tasmania, via the thrice-weekly ferry which makes the trip across Bass Strait from Melbourne in fourteen hours.

Rocks at Mersey Bluff near the mouth of the river are covered with Aboriginal carvings and the site is among the most significant in the study of the culture of Tasmania's natives. A cultural and arts center nearby features a display of Aboriginal life. Launceston is a further 100 km (62 miles) to the east.

HOW TO GET THERE

All Tasbureau coach tours follow the west coast route and Tasmania Redline, which offers a 14-day Tassie Pass coach ticket for visitors, covers the route daily.

LAUNCESTON

Tasmania's second largest city is otherwise known as The Garden City because of its numerous parks and gardens in which European trees such as ash, oaks and elms thrive. It is an excellent base for exploring the northern part of Tasmania, and also has many attractions in its own right.

Launceston's outstanding natural beauty spot, only a few minutes' walk from the center, is **Cataract Gorge**, a canyon through which the South Esk River plunges - with spectacular feroc-

OPPOSITE Sunset at Bicheno, busy little fishing port and charming old holiday resort.

ity after heavy rain. A walking path follows the cliff face and a 300 m (985 ft) chairlift, the world's largest single-span lift, offers a breathtaking ride over the waters. Several walks have been laid out through the gorge.

The natural beauty of Launceston - founded only a few months after Hobart - is interspersed with a variety of historic buildings, a number of which stand in St John and George streets.

The best-known commercial attraction is the **Penny Royal World** on Paterson Street, which recreates the industry of colonial days. A watermill has been restored to working order, along with a cornmill, windmill, gunpowder mill, cannon foundry and arsenal. Tasmania's second casino, the **Country Club**, operates at Prospect Vale on the southern fringe of the city.

Tourist Information
The Tasbureau office is on the corner of St John and Paterson streets, tel: (003) 322488, and the National Trust has an information center at The Old Umbrella Shop, 60 George Street.

HOTELS AND MOTELS

Country Club Casino, Country Club Avenue, Prospect Vale. Tel: (003) 448855. 120 units and suites. Rates: expensive.
Balmoral Motor Inn, 19 York Street. Tel: (003) 318000. 36 rooms. Rates: average.
Old Launceston Hotel, 107 Brisbane Street. Tel: (003) 319211. 16 rooms. Rates: average.
Windmill Hill Tourist Lodge, 22 High Street. Tel: (003) 319337. 6 rooms. Rates: budget.
Royal Hotel, 90 George Street. Tel: (003) 312526. 16 rooms. Rates: budget.

RESTAURANTS

The Aristocrat, corner of Paterson and Charles streets. Souvlaki and braised hare are highlights of a Greek Menu.
Old Masters, 58 Elizabeth Street. French cuisine with excellent sorbets and ice creams to end the meal.

ABOVE Ringaroo River in Tasmania's north-east. OPPOSITE A jolly boat ride at Launceston's Penny Royal World.

HOW TO GET THERE

Australian Airlines and Ansett fly in from the mainland, and it is 25 minutes flying time from Hobart. Redline coaches take three hours from Hobart.

STATELY HOMES

The countryside around Launceston is dotted with grand mansions built by rich property owners, and charming villages with a distinctly English flavour - a similarity strengthened by village greens and quiet rural roads lined by hawthorn hedges.

The most imposing of Tasmania's stately homes, **Clarendon**, stands in peaceful grounds at Nile, about 25 km (15 miles) south of Launceston on the road through Evandale. The gracious Georgian house, dominated by its magnificent portico, has been restored to its former distinction by the National Trust.

The Trust was formed in Tasmania especially to buy and preserve **Franklin House**, built by convicts and once a leading school in the colony. It stands alongside the Bass Highway on its approach into Launceston.

Entally, in the village of Hadspen 15 km (9 miles) southwest of the city, is preserved and furnished to reconstruct the life of the 1820s when the house was built. All three homes are open to the public.

HOW TO GET THERE

Inquire at Launceston's Tasbureau office for tours.

THE EAST COAST

Tasmania is not well endowed with the Australian outdoors trilogy of sun, surf and sand; the nearest you get to it is on the east coast, where there is a string of small resorts.

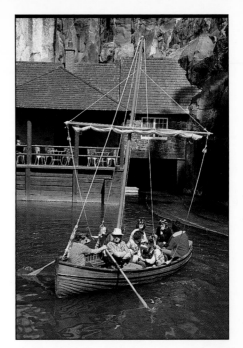

The Tasman Highway, the 435 km (270 miles) coastal road between Launceston and Hobart, loops through the northeast corner, skirting the rocky bastion of the Ben Lomond plateau and reaching the coast at **St Helens**, a former whaling village and now a small-fishing port/resort whose population of 800 swells ten-fold during the summer. A game fishing fleet hunts tuna and shark.

The beaches at **Scamander**, 20 km (13 miles) south, are said to be the best along the coast. **Bicheno**, another 60 km (37 miles) down the coast, was a shelter for early whalers and sealers and still derives its living from the sea, but now the boats catch crayfish. A modest grave near Silver Sands is that of a nineteenth century heroine, Waubedar, an Aboriginal woman who saved two sealers during a storm. Snowdrops flower on the grave every year. **Sea Life Centre** displays hundreds of kinds of Tasmanian marine life in its tanks.

The south road through the small town of Swansea hugs the shore for 20 km (13 miles), with views across to the

Freycinet Peninsula, a national park of red granite peaks and spectacular rocky coastline.

On the way back to Hobart a detour of about 14 km (9 miles) near Sorell brings you to the showpiece colonial village of **Richmond,** little changed over a century, with Australia's earliest Catholic church (1837) and oldest bridge (1825). Legend has it that the ghost of a brutal overseer thrown into the river by convicts haunts the bridge, so watch your step.

HOW TO GET THERE

A bus service runs along the coast, and

Richmond is included in tours from Hobart.

MIDLAND HIGHWAY

The direct Hobart-Launceston road is Tasmania's main artery. It bypasses many of the historic villages along its route, allowing them to revert to a peace which was lost with the advent of motor vehicles. Most townships have histories as coaching stops and military depots and are abundant in colonial character.

Bagdad, 37 km (23 miles) north of Hobart, is only one of several southern settlements with names from the Bible or *The Arabian Nights*: the two books said to be carried by an explorer in the area.

In the opinion of many visitors, the village of **Ross,** 120 km (75 miles) north of Hobart, is the prettiest place in the State. Its dominant feature is a convict-built stone bridge decorated with fine carvings – the prisoner responsible for the work was given his freedom as a reward.

The village is splendidly preserved and almost a living museum, its wide main street lined with shady trees, historic homes and public buildings, many of which have been restored. A deer park and wildlife sanctuary are a short drive away.

Perth, on the highway only 20 km (13 miles) south of Launceston, also has strong nineteenth century connections. The historic **Leather Bottel Inn** has been converted into an excellent restaurant.

HOW TO GET THERE

Tasmania Redline runs several Hobart-Launceston buses a day, and the journey takes three hours.

OFF THE BEATEN TRACK

LAND OF LAKES

Least used of the roads between north and south Tasmania is the most wild – the scenic Lakes Highway, which follows the Derwent Valley and then climbs up to the windswept central plateau with its scurrying cloud, moorland and thrusting mountain grandeur.

The eastern portion, the **Land of Three Hundred Lakes,** is made up of countless tarns, rivers and lakes teeming with the trout that make the region one of the world's classic fishing grounds. Tasbureau can arrange fishing holidays; accommodation is in tents or chalets.

Many of the large lakes feed water to

ydro-electricity schemes linked to ivers which flow off the plateau. Tasmania has harnessed its waters to more han half a dozen complex schemes there are ten power stations on the Dervent scheme alone). Some stations are open to the public and provide a fascinating insight into how the water is turned into power.

The lake country can be very bleak for long stretches of the year, but spring sees it burst into life with wildflowers, and also sees the first of the season's anglers.

HOW TO GET THERE

Turn south at Deloraine, leave the Midland Highway at Melton Mowbray, or the Lyell Highway at Hamilton or Bronte. It's about 150 km (93 miles) from Deloraine to Melton Mowbray across the plateau. Contact Tasbureau for current tours.

WALKERS' PARADISE

Tasmania's magnificently rugged scenery attracts hikers from all over Australia, and all twelve national parks are laced with walking trails.

By far the most popular is the 85 km (53 mile) five-day trek though **Cradle Mountain-Lake St Clair National Park,** on the western side of the central plateau. The Overland Track skirts the 17 km (11 mile) long lake, scooped out long ago by glaciers, and winds through forested valleys and over mountain ridges.

For the most hardy and competent backpackers there is the tough challenge of the **Port Davey-South Coast Track,** around the rough and ocean-battered southwest shoreline of the State. The trail leads through the heart of the **South West National Park** wilderness, crosses glacier-scarred mountains and river systems, follows a path through dense forest and can take almost two weeks to

negotiate. The track extends between the southern end of Lake Pedder and Hastings, on the D'Entrecasteaux Channel. The region is the bleakest in Australia and the second wettest, but with even reasonable weather it is a memorable trek. However, walking parties must register with police or park rangers.

HOW TO GET THERE

Special transport to the two parks leaves Hobart, Launceston and Devonport, with one Launceston service operating direct from the airport to Cradle Mountain Park. Ask Tasbureau for details.

NORTHWEST

While in the north, attempt to visit the northwest corner along the Bass Highway, where the coast's pastoral land turns a distinctive chocolate color when ploughed. The terrain climbs steeply to forested mountains and high heaths where tropical plants thrive in sheltered areas.

The Nut, with the town of **Stanley** at its foot, is an unmistakable landmark on the coast, and from its table top it is possible to see many kilometers in each direction. The 136 m (450 ft) headland is a volcanic plug created when lava exploded through a fault more than 10 million years ago.

From The Nut you can look 20 km (13 miles) eastward to Rocky Cape, where a national park contains Aboriginal paintings and several rare kinds of orchids.

HOW TO GET THERE

Day tours leave from Launceston and Devonport, and a weekday bus service operates to Smithton.

OPPOSITE The beautiful convict-built bridge at Ross. The convict who carried out the carving received his freedom as a reward.

Northern Territory

A Last Frontier

THE ISOLATED NORTH

Picture Australia in your mind, and the Northern Territory will probably come closest to what you see. Daunting distances, the unremitting Outback, the arid Red Centre, Ayers Rock, and cattle stations as big as Wales or Massachusetts (where round-up is done by motorcycle and helicopter), the Flying Doctor and lonely, sun-bleached one-pub townships.

This is Australia's last frontier and the Territorians work hard at preserving their image. The isolation has forged a muscular sense of independence and they are not going to have those know-all southerners (which means everyone else in Australia) telling them how to run things.

There may only be around 130,000 people in the Territory, more than 80,000 in Darwin and Alice Springs and the rest scattered over an area which is one-sixth of the Australian land mass, but they believe in making their collective voice heard. Communications have improved since World War II and brought the Territory closer to the remainder of Australia. But it is still a long way from anywhere else.

Best time to visit the Top End in the north around Darwin is between April and October, during the Dry, when the days are sunny and the evenings balmy. During the Wet, monsoonal downpours and high humidity make life miserable, even for the locals. Alice Springs and the Centre to the south can be unbearably hot in summer, but are pleasantly warm the remainder of the year.

DARWIN

The capital, on the shore of the Timor Sea, is a new city, all sparkling and shiny. The old one was torn from its foundations in December 1974 by Cy-

clone Tracy, which left 66 dead in her furious wake. Half of the 11,000 homes were destroyed and many historic buildings disappeared forever.

But the city has been reborn and the population is now larger than before the cyclone. People forced to evacuate have returned to rebuild, and many newcomers from the south who came to help with construction have stayed. The lusty fertility of the tropics has restored the gardens with a riot of colorful bougainvillea, frangipani and poinsettia, suburbs have been rebuilt, and the

physical scars of Tracy have all but vanished.

The revival has been facilitated by the Territory achieving self-government, bringing in a whole new infrastructure of government. The new focus on the area, and its independent status, has also improved the economy and made Darwin dynamic and affluent.

Tourist Information
The Territory Government Tourist Bureau is at 31 Smith Street Mall. Tel: (089) 816611.

TOURING DARWIN

The city is by far the smallest of the nation's capitals, but the number of the

OPPOSITE A road train, workhorse of the north.
ABOVE Hand-feeding stock during a drought.

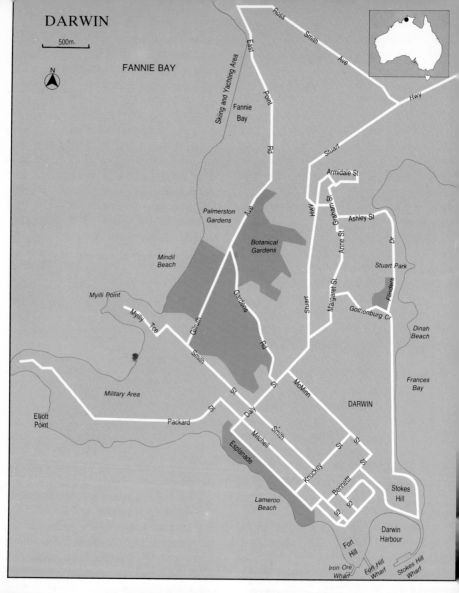

DARWIN

500m.

N

FANNIE BAY

Ross

Smith

Ave

Hwy

East

Point

Skiing and Yachting Area

Fannie
Bay

Rd

Stuart

Armidale St

Graham St

Ashley St

Anne St

Hwy

Palmerston
Gardens

Ave

Botanical
Gardens

Magaren St

Stuart Park

Flinders

Dr

Mindil
Beach

Gothenburg Cr

Dinah
Beach

Myilli Point

Myilly

Tce

Gilruth

Gardens

Stuart

Rd

Frances
Bay

Smith

St

McMinn

DARWIN

Military Area

St

Daly

Smith

St

St

Elliott
Point

Packard

St

Mitchell

St

St

Esplanade

Knuckey

Bennett

St

Stokes
Hill

Lameroo
Beach

St

Darwin
Harbour

Fort
Hill

Iron Ore
Wharf

Fort Hill
Wharf

Stokes Hill
Wharf

sights worth seeing are sufficiently scattered to warrant signing on for a bus tour.

Wander around the harbor end of town where most of the historic buildings which survived Tracy are to be found. You cannot go into the Administrator's House on its prime piece of real estate overlooking the harbor, but you can peek through the gate for a look at a true survivor. The century-old building has lived through Japanese air attacks and a succession of cyclones. The new octagonal Anglican cathedral just along the Esplanade was designed around the original porch, all that was left standing after Tracy. The Chinese community was not so fortunate, its temple being totally destroyed. However the new building, in Woods Street, is open to the public.

Bus tours will take you further afield. The **Botanic Gardens** have a collection of hundreds of tropical plants, and an amphitheater that is the setting for musical events varying from ballet to Aboriginal dances. A superb collection of Aboriginal artifacts and oceania art has been collected by the **Museum of Arts and Sciences**, a handsome new venture at Fannie Bay. Also on some city tours is a **crocodile farm** 40 km (25 miles) down the Stuart Highway. Here more than four thousand of the reptiles can be seen at various stages of growth from egg to jaw-snapping monster.

Not quite so far out of town, **Yarrawonga Park** is a wildlife garden inhabited by buffaloes, crocodiles, emus and snakes and is a great favorite with wildlife enthusiasts and family groups.

SHOPPING

Darwin is THE place to buy your Aboriginal artifacts. The largest collection is at the **Aboriginal Heritage Gallery** in Smith Street mall, where there are woven baskets, weapons, bark paintings and other examples of Aboriginal

skills. Also in the mall is the **Studio Star Art Gallery**, showing paintings and pottery by Territorians.

DARWIN BY NIGHT

Darwin likes to think of itself as being different, and it's the only place in Australia where you can while away the evening looking for crocodiles by spotlight. The tour also includes watching killer snakes being fed at a reptile park, so it's probably not for the faint-hearted.

The other choices of nightlife are more orthodox, with most of the action taking place at the pyramid-shaped **Diamond Beach Casino Hotel**. If you don't want to gamble, enjoy yourself watching the the cabaret or discoing at **Crystals. Fannies**, in Edmund Street, rocks until dawn every morning, and you can also rage at the **Beachcomber** at the Telford Top End Hotel.

A word of warning when you go socializing in Darwin. The locals feel that it is not possible to have a good time without a can of beer in one hand. So don't try to out-drink them; they get lots of practice, and boast of Darwin being the beer-drinking capital of Australia.

Darwin has about fifty restaurants to choose from. Try a buffalo steak - the animals run wild in the Territory and are considered a nuisance - or barramundi, a succulent fish found only in northern waters.

HOTELS AND MOTELS

Diamond Beach Hotel Casino, Gilruth Avenue, Mindil Beach. Tel: (089) 817755. 106 rooms and suites. Rates: expensive.
Darwin Travelodge, 122 Esplanade.

OPPOSITE Darwin's casino hotel, and Aboriginal art and weaving in Kakadu National Park.

Tel: (089) 815 5388. 183 rooms and suites. Rates: average.

Poinciana Motel, corner Mclachlan and Mitchell streets. Tel: (089) 818111. 49 units. Rates: average.

Don Hotel Motel, 12 Cavenagh Street. Tel: (089) 815311. 40 units. Rates: average.

Lameroo Lodge, 69 Mitchell Street. Tel: (089) 819733. 304 rooms. Rates: budget.

Larrakeyah Lodge, 50 Mitchell Street. Tel: (089) 812933. 56 rooms. Rates: budget.

RESTAURANTS

Le Sommet, Diamond Beach. Superb international cuisine.

Bagus, Pavonia Place. Indonesian menu, specializing in Balinese dishes.

Stingers, Mitchell Street. Specializes in seafood.

Safari Bistro, Travelodge, The Esplanade. Blackboard menu features buff steaks and barramundi.

HOW TO GET THERE

By air it's four and a half hours from Adelaide or Brisbane, and eight and a half hours from Sydney. Coaches take 49 hours from Brisbane, 60 hours from Perth and 21 hours from Alice Springs.

KAKADU NATIONAL PARK

The park is the showplace of the Top End - a spectacular and ancient wilderness of dramatic scenery, home of hundreds of species of birds and animals, and a treasure house of Aboriginal art and lore belonging to the oldest culture in the world. In all, it is one of the world's great parks, which is why it has been placed on the highly prestigious

World Heritage List.

The park is 250 km (156 miles) east of Darwin on the western fringe of Arnhem Land, the bridge over which the Aboriginals entered Australia tens of thousands of years ago when the continent was connected to the lands to the north.

The art galleries or rock paintings are a window on the past, a record of the culture and beliefs of the Dreamtime, the Aboriginal legends which tell of the birth of Australia and the Aboriginal

ABOVE Arltunga goldrush ghost town, and Katherine Gorge. OPPOSITE Aboriginal children playing in Arnhem Land; relaxing in the Katherine River.

people. More than 300 galleries have been found by the white man, and it is estimated that at least another 1,000 are known only to the Aborigines. The most easily reached are found at Obiri Rock and Nourlangie Rock and make fascinating excursions into the prehistoric past.

The park takes in a broad flood plain backed by the high ramparts of the Armhem Land escarpment. In the Wet, majestic waterfalls thunder off the plateau, with the 200 m (650 ft) drop of the Jim Jim Falls the most breathtaking.

In the Dry the waters recede to a series of lagoons and billabongs which attract thousands of birds. Crocodiles patrol the muddy rivers and buffaloes gaze balefully at intruders.

HOW TO GET THERE

A selection of tours leaves from Darwin. The boat trip on the croc-infested South Alligator River is a day to remember and definitely shouldn't be missed.

There is only one main road in the Territory, the Stuart Highway, which runs 1,530 km (950 miles) from Darwin to Alice Springs, and then another 290 km (180 miles) to the South Australian border. So let's head south for the Red Centre. Known in these parts simply as "the track," the two-lane road passes scrawny woodland and savannah, your landscape for the next several hundred kilometers. Adelaide River, 112 km (70

miles) out of Darwin, was a headquarters for Australian and American troops during World War II and Australia's only mainland war cemetery is just off the highway. Also buried here are civilians killed in the Japanese bombing of Darwin.

The almost-deserted old gold town of **Pine Creek,** 132 km (82 miles) south, had a population of 30,000 a century ago – now it has just over 200, some of whom still prospect for gold in the surrounding hills. Debris of the heady times and remains of a Chinatown can still be seen.

The only town of any size in the Top End outside Darwin is **Katherine,** 321 km (200 miles) south of Darwin and famous for its gorges. Actually it's only one gorge, divided into a series of 13 canyons, confined within dramatic 70 m (230 ft) walls which constantly change

color according to the light and time of day. In the second gorge is the sheer face of **Jedda's Leap,** where legend has it a couple jumped to their deaths because they were not allowed to wed. You can join a boat ride up the first two canyons which is the best way to appreciate the gorge's awesome beauty.

About an hour south of Katherine is one of nature's little bonuses. If the heat and endless road have become too exhausting for you, jump into the brilliantly clear thermal pool at **Mataranka.** The spring supports a small pocket of palms and lush tropical forest in a landscape otherwise lean of vegetation and makes a delightful break from the rigors of the road.

Hour after hour of flat tableland is relieved only by a handful of tiny settlements. The thin woodland gives way to the scrub and redness of the inland at **Renner Springs,** 500 km (310 miles) south of Katherine, the change marking the limit of the monsoon.

Tennant Creek, another one and a half hours down the track, was the scene of Australia's last full-blooded gold rush in 1932 and even today one mine is still producing. The creek itself is 11 km (7 miles) out of town because many years ago convenience overrode good intention. A cart carrying materials for a pub to be built at the creek became bogged in the mud, so the publican unloaded the wagon and built the pub on the spot. The miners chose to build their town near the pub rather than near the water supply of the creek! The 507 km (315 mile) journey to Alice Springs takes you past the huge strewn boulders of the **Devil's Marbles,** which Aborigines believe are eggs laid by a secret serpent, and alongside **Central Mount Stuart,** a low round hill which as near as makes no difference is the geographical center of the continent.

THE ALICE

Maybe it's because the name has a certain ring about it, or maybe it's the isolation of the place, but the capital of the Centre has always had a romantic image in Australian minds as a little town a million miles from anywhere struggling along with only the basic necessities of life and none of the luxuries.

All this might have been true up

196

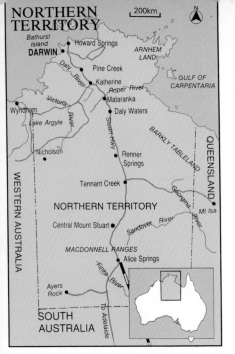

NORTHERN TERRITORY

200km

N

Bathurst Island

DARWIN

Howard Springs

ARNHEM LAND

Pine Creek

Katherine

Roper River

Mataranka

Daly Waters

GULF OF CARPENTARIA

Wyndham

Lake Argyle

Victoria River

Daly River

Nicholson

Renner Springs

BARKLY TABLELAND

QUEENSLAND

Tennant Creek

NORTHERN TERRITORY

Central Mount Stuart

Sandover River

Georgina River

Mt Isa

MACDONNELL RANGES

Alice Springs

WESTERN AUSTRALIA

Ayers Rock

Finke River

SOUTH AUSTRALIA

To Adelaide

about 20 years ago when the population had struggled to reach 4,000 and The Alice survived as an uneventful cow town and a railhead to move cattle south.

Since then tourism has discovered the Centre, and times are booming. Population has increased five-fold since the '60s, there are luxury motels, caravan parks, restaurants which serve something more than the traditional steak and eggs, and even a casino to cater for the 150,000 visitors who pass through each year. A cavalcade of buses grinds through the town each day, streamlined air-conditioned trains roll in from Sydney and Adelaide, and jets drop in from all the State capitals.

The reason for The Alice's being, an historic relay station on the Adelaide-Darwin Overland Telegraph line, stands next to a waterhole four kilometers (two and a half miles) out of town and has become a favorite tourist attraction. These were the first buildings in the Centre, the township came later.

The Alice has always been important to the Territory, and some of the innovations which eased the hardships of Outback life originated here. Buried under a boulder a few minutes out of town is the body of missionary John Flynn, who played a major role in forming the world-famous Flying Doctor Service, which brings medical aid to remote properties and townships. The simple hospital he built stands in the main street, near a church dedicated to him. The service also brought radio to the Outback and today the benefits of communications are used in the School of the Air. The Alice school was the first of its type in the world when opened in the 1950s and in term time you can listen in as teachers talk by radio to pupils scattered over vast distances.

The Alice huddles in the bowl of the **MacDonnell Ranges**, whose scenic red-walled gorges form the main natural attraction of the region. The road west passes one canyon after another; the narrow crevice of **Standley Chasm, Simpsons Gap** with its rock pool and shy wallabies, and **Ormiston Gorge**.

Much of the countryside in the Centre is Aboriginal reserve, so if you plan to visit any out-of-the-way places, first check to see whether you need a permit or are allowed in. One in four people in Central Australia is an Aborigine, a fact most evident on the streets of Alice Springs. Two reserves are just outside town, while many others live on out-stations or in tiny communities dotted around the inland.

Tourist Information

For anything you want to know about the area, visit the Government Tourist Bureau at 51 Todd Street. Tel: (089) 521299.

HOW TO GET THERE

Unless you fly, it's a long way to The Alice. Coaches take 26 hours from

OPPOSITE An artist's impressions of Alice Springs decorate the wall of the market in the town's shopping center.

Adelaide and 43 hours from Brisbane. The New Ghan train takes 24 hours for its weekly run from Adelaide, while The Alice train from Sydney takes two days for the trip.

AYERS ROCK

This is what visitors to the Centre come to see. Ask any non-Australian which one natural landmark in Australia springs to mind first and chances are the reply will be: "Ayers Rock." Along with Sydney Harbour Bridge it's internationally synonymous with the nation. The famous domed silhouette is recognized world-wide.

The Rock is big and thrusting, rising 384 m (1,260 ft) out of the mulga plain and stretching almost nine kilometers (six miles) around the base. A brooding, mysterious atmosphere surrounds it. It constantly changes color depending on the time of day and weather. On sunny days it can be any tint of red or orange,

while in wet weather it can be black or white or any shade between. In the evening photographers make pilgrimages out into the desert to capture it in a superb sunset.

The flanks are etched with deep gullies which gush with waterfalls after rain, and each feature has a place in Aboriginal folklore. Its importance in the Aboriginal spiritual framework is known only to Aborigines themselves.

Potholes are marks of spears, a boulder was once a body. A watercourse follows a track left by a dying warrior as he crawled away. The Aborigines call it Uluru – a mystical name for a magical place.

The climb to the top and down again takes 90 minutes, but it is not easy, and can be dangerous. A chain handrail helps climbers past the more difficult stretches. About 75,000 begin the climb

each year, and most reach the top. However many turn back at the "chicken rock," so don't be too embarrassed if you don't make it.

Going to Ayers Rock used to be something of a challenge, involving a 240 km (150 mile) drive along a dirt track, but now civilization has come to the landmark. It's bitumen every inch of the 442 km (275 miles) from The Alice, and two new and spankingly modern motels with a combined total of 400 rooms and suites provide every civilized comfort a tourist can desire.

HOW TO GET THERE

There is a daily bus service between The Alice and Ayers Rock and a variety of day-trips and long packages. You can also pay the Rock a flying visit for the day.

OPPOSITE The Olgas. ABOVE Trailers piggy-backing, baby-backpacking in Ormiston Gorge. LEFT Standley Chasm.

Travelers' Tips

More than a score of international airlines fly into Australia. Most enter through Sydney and Melbourne, although others arrive - less frequently - at Perth, Darwin, Brisbane and Hobart. All the airports are conveniently close to the city centers, with Melbourne's Tullamarine - about a half-hour drive along a freeway - the most distant.

The approach path into Sydney is surpassed by few others, and passengers on the left side of the aircraft can look down upon the harbor, the Opera House and Harbour Bridge.

Don't forget to keep A$20 in your pocket when preparing to leave the country. A departure tax of this amount (in Australian currency only) must be paid by all departing passengers. The tax is at present paid at the airport, but efforts are being made to incorporate it into the air fare or devise some other, more convenient method of collection.

The major international carriers can be contacted at:

Air New Zealand
Adelaide, tel: (08) 212 3544
Brisbane, tel: (07) 229 3044
Melbourne, tel: (03) 654 3311
Perth, tel: (09) 325 1099
Sydney, tel: (02) 233 6888

British Airways
Adelaide, tel: (08) 212 1022
Brisbane, tel: (07) 229 3166
Canberra, tel: (062) 476322
Hobart, tel: (002) 347156
Melbourne, tel: (03) 602 3500
Perth, tel: (09) 322 6433
Sydney, tel: (02) 232 1777

Canadian Pacific
Melbourne, tel: (03) 625457
Sydney, tel: (02) 268 1861

Cathay Pacific
Adelaide, tel: (08) 212 4483
Brisbane, tel: (07) 229 9344
Melbourne, tel: (03) 670 0156
Perth, tel: (09) 322 1377
Sydney, tel: (02) 231 5122

Continental Airlines
Adelaide, tel: (08) 212 6155
Brisbane, tel: (07) 221 1474
Canberra, tel: (062) 317981
Melbourne, tel: (03) 602 5377
Perth, tel: (09) 481 1688
Sydney, tel: (02) 290 1133

Japan Airlines
Brisbane, tel: (07) 229 9916
Melbourne, tel: (03) 654 2733
Sydney, tel: (02) 233 4500

Malaysian Airline System
Adelaide, tel: (08) 516171
Brisbane, tel: (07) 229 9888
Melbourne, tel: (03) 663 2445
Perth, tel: (09) 325 9188
Sydney, tel: (02) 232 3377

Qantas
Adelaide, tel: (08) 218 8418
Brisbane, tel: (07) 224 3711
Canberra, tel: (062) 481411
Darwin, tel: (089) 823312
Hobart, tel: (002) 345700
Melbourne, tel: (03) 602 6026
Perth, tel: (09) 327 6222
Sydney, tel: (02) 236 3636

Singapore Airlines
Adelaide, tel: (08) 212 3656
Brisbane, tel: (07) 713171
Canberra, tel: (062) 474122
Hobart, tel: (002) 347955
Melbourne, tel: (03) 602 4555
Perth, tel: (09) 322 24422
Sydney, tel: (02) 231 3522

United Airlines
Adelaide, tel: (08) 512821
Melbourne, tel: (03) 654 4488
Sydney, tel: (02) 237 8696

INTERNAL FLIGHTS

The two major internal airlines, the Government-owned Australia Airlines and privately owned Ansett Airlines, operate services to more than 100 cities, towns and tourist centers. East-West Airlines also flies an interstate schedule, while a number of regional and feeder companies fly to smaller destinations. Apart from the normal first class, business and economy fares, Australian Airlines and Ansett also offer certain discount fares. Visitors traveling on a Qantas excursion ticket get 30 percent off internal flights on Australia Airlines or Ansett, providing their domestic flight is more than 1,000 km.

The main office phone numbers are:
Ansett Airlines
Adelaide, tel: (08) 217 7222
Brisbane, tel: (07) 228 8222
Canberra, tel: (062) 465111
Darwin, tel: (089) 803211
Hobart, tel: (002) 380800
Melbourne, tel: (03) 668 1211
Perth, tel: (09) 325 0201
Sydney, tel: (02) 268 1555

Australian Airlines
Adelaide, tel: (08) 216 1911
Brisbane, tel: (07) 332011
Canberra, tel: (062) 461811
Darwin, tel: (089) 823311
Hobart, tel: (002) 383511
Melbourne, tel: (03) 345 1333
Perth, tel: (09) 323 8444
Sydney, tel: (02) 669 9555

VISAS

All visitors require a passport and visa to enter Australia, except for New Zealanders, who do not require a visa. The visa will state the permitted length of stay, which is usually a maximum of six months. If you wish to stay longer contact the nearest office of the Commonwealth Government's Department of Immigration and Ethnic Affairs. Application for a visa should be made to Australian consular offices, which can be found in 74 countries around the world.

CUSTOMS ALLOWANCES

Visitors over 18 years of age may bring in 200 cigarettes or 250 gm (9 oz) of cigars or tobacco, and one liter (1.75 pints) of alcohol. Because of the importance of protecting the agricultural industry, Australia is extremely strict about the importation of insects, animals, plants, seeds and certain foodstuffs. The continent is free from many overseas pests and diseases and makes every effort to make sure that this continues. The interior of every aircraft is sprayed upon arrival, so if you suffer from any respiratory ailment it is wise to cover your mouth and nose.

CURRENCY

Australia uses a decimal system of currency, expressed in dollars and cents. Coins come in copper denominations of 1 cent and 2 cents, and silver coins in 5 cents, 10 cents, 20 cents and 50 cents. A golden-colored $1 coin has recently been introduced which is only slightly larger than the 10 cent coin, so make sure that you do not confuse the two when handling money.

Notes are in different colors and available in denominations of $2, $5, $10, $20, $50 and $100.

Travelers' checks present no problems and can be easily cashed at international airports, banks, hotels and motels. Internationally-recognized credit cards are also accepted. American Express, Mastercard, Diners Club, Visa and Carte Blanche are the most frequently used. There is no limit on the amount of foreign currency which can be brought into the country.

Banks are open 9:30 am - 4 pm Monday to Thursday, and until 5 pm on Friday.

GETTING AROUND

Because of the size of Australia, air travel is the most convenient way of seeing the continent. There are also complex rail and coach (bus) networks

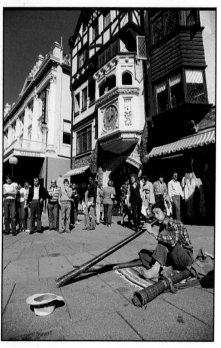

stretching across the nation which allow you to see more of the countryside.

BY RAIL

Australian trains are not the fastest in the world and in terms of speed come nowhere near matching the super-fast expresses of Europe or the *shinkansen* bullet trains of Japan. (The Sydney-Melbourne overnight sleeper, for instance, takes 13 hours for the journey at an average of 67 km (41 miles) an hour.)

Interstate services are, however, comfortable and well-serviced with air-conditioning, sleeping cabins, dining and buffet cars and showers. Trains such as the Sydney to Perth transcontinental Indian-Pacific even have a piano and videotaped television on board. On the MotoRail services it is possible to take your car with you.

The main line runs up the eastern seaboard from Melbourne as far north as Cairns; with lines connecting westward from Sydney and Melbourne to Adelaide in South Australia, Alice Springs in the Northern Territory and Perth in Western Australia. Australia has some wonderful railway journeys acknowledged by enthusiasts the world over. A number of them have romantic names to match. These include The Vinelander between Melbourne and the wine-producing area of Mildura; The Prospector from Perth to the goldfields city of Kalgoorlie; The Ghan (short for the Afghan camel drivers of the Outback last century) between Adelaide and Alice Springs; and The Sunlander from Brisbane to Cairns.

State railways can be reached at: **New South Wales**: Corner of York and Market streets, Sydney. Tel: (02) 290 4743.

Queensland: Information and bookings through the Queensland Government Travel Centre, 196 Adelaide Street, Brisbane. Tel: (07) 312211 or interstate offices.

Victoria: 589 Collins Street, Melbourne. Tel: (03) 619 1500.

Special Fares

Visitors who intend to travel extensively by rail should invest in a first-class Austrailpass or a second-class Budget. Each is an excellent bargain and **must be bought outside Australia**, although they can be extended when you are in Australia. The passes cover any period between 14 days and three months, and give the purchaser unlimited travel anywhere in the country, including the city and suburban services. They do not cover such extras as restaurant car and sleeping berth charges. Four of the State rail systems also offer special tickets for unlimited travel on their own networks for varying periods, in one case up to a year. Queensland has its Sunshine Rail Pass; New South Wales the Nurail and Rover tickets; Victoria the Rail-Away tickets and Western Australia its Westrailpass.

A discount CAPER (Customer Advance Purchase Excursion Rail) fare is also available between Sydney and Melbourne and Adelaide and Melbourne. The (railroad) systems also operate a wide range of touring services, including package tours of several days' duration.

All interstate rail services are linked to a centralized booking system, so you can book all your journeys at one place, whether it be a rail office, tourist bureau or travel agent. Even if you do not want to take advantage of the various concession tickets which are available, train travel in Australia is very reasonably priced.

The Sunshine Rail Pass costs: first class, 14 days $231; 21 days $284; a month $347; economy, 14 days $152, 21 days $184, a month $231. Nurail Pass (14 days, travel economy or first class) $110. Daily Rover $4.50; Weekly Rover $22.50 V/Line Rail-Away (14 days travel): first class $75, economy $55. Westrailpass 14 days $144, a month $226, 3 months $617.

BY BUS

The many express coach - or in other words bus - services available around Australia provide efficient and economical links between big cities and towns. Buses are air-conditioned with washrooms and adjustable seats, which is just as well considering that some of the journeys are of marathon propor-

tions. Perth to Darwin, for example, entails a trip of 60 hours.

The two leading companies are Ansett Pioneer and Greyhound and both operate extensive express services Australia-wide. Deluxe, AAT King's and Australian Pacific, as well as Across Australia Coachlines, also operate coasts-to-coast; while smaller companies meet the needs of specific regions of the country. Money-saving tickets which give unlimited travel for various durations are Ansett Pioneer's Aussiepass, Greyhound's Eaglepass (which carries some discounts), the Deluxe Koala Pass, Westrail's road-rail pass, and Tasman Red Line's Tassiepass.

The coach operators also offer hundreds of tours; the most exciting being Australia-wide trips which can take nearly two months and call at all the most scenic areas of the continent, and camping tours which particularly appeal to passengers planning Outback trips. The tours are escorted by staff, but passengers look after their own tents and can help prepare meals. Setting up camp in the dusk of the Outback and swapping yarns around a campfire with the silence of the continent all around and the star-studded canopy above is an experience to treasure.

A wide range of tours leaves from each capital city. For instance, there is a month-long tour originating from Melbourne, Sydney and Brisbane, which travels up the eastern seaboard calling at the exhilarating Gold Coast, cruising through islands on the Great Barrier Reef and exploring the lush rain forest of Northern Queensland before heading inland through the remote Gulf Country and Mt Isa into the Northern Territory. Highlights of the tour are visits to Kakadu National Park, one of the world's most beautiful parks, and Ayers Rock,

OPPOSITE Showing how it's done on a didgeridoo, an extremely difficult instrument to play.

the giant ancient dome which rears out of the plain in the Red Centre of the continent. The tour continues south through the center, calling at the famous little opal mining town of Coober Pedy before heading back towards the east coast.

A favorite destination for coach tours out of Adelaide is the Flinders Ranges, a few hundred kilometers to the north. The jagged ancient ranges are rich in scenery and Aboriginal lore.

To tour the most remote part of Australia, the rugged and time-worn northwest corner of the continent that is the Kimberleys, visitors can fly from Perth and pick up their coach at the old pearling town of Broome. Tours visit the spectacularly beautiful gorges of the region, and some itineraries go on into the Northern Territory.

Tours can be booked through travel agents or State tourism organizations, while the two major companies - which operate central booking systems - can be contacted at:

Ansett Pioneer
Adelaide: 101 Franklin Street. Tel: (08) 512075.
Brisbane: 16 Ann Street. Tel: (07) 226 1184.
Canberra: Corner of Northbourne Avenue and Ipima Street. Tel: (062) 456624.
Darwin: 63 Smith Street. Tel: (089) 816433.
Hobart: 96 Harrington Street. Tel: (002) 344577.
Melbourne: Corner of Franklin and Swanston streets. Tel: (03) 668 2422.
Perth: 26 St Georges Terrace. Tel: (09) 325 8855.
Sydney: Oxford Square. Tel: (02) 268 1881.

Greyhound
Adelaide, 111 Franklin Street. Tel: (08) 212 1777.
Brisbane, 79 Melbourne Street, South

Brisbane. Tel: (07) 240 9333.
Canberra, 65 Northbourne Avenue. Tel: (062) 572659.
Darwin, 67 Mitchell Street. Tel: (089) 818510.
Hobart, Tasbureau, 80 Elizabeth Street. Tel: (002) 346911.
Melbourne, 667 Bourke Street. Tel: (03) 6144240.
Perth, Wellington Street bus station. Tel: (09) 478 1122.
Sydney, Oxford Square. Tel: (02) 268 1414.

BY CAR

Avis, Hertz and Budget are the leading car rental companies with outlets at major airports and agents across the country, although there are many smaller local businesses. A deposit is usually requested when picking up the vehicle, and the vehicle does not necessarily have to be returned to the place of pick-up. Compulsory third-party insurance is included in the rental price, and comprehensive insurance is available for an extra charge. Age restrictions apply to most rentals, with 21 usually the minimum age. Caravans and four-wheel drive vehicles can also be hired, and are particularly popular in the conveniently small state of Tasmania.

It cannot be emphasized too strongly that driving in the Outback is a specialized form of motoring - you must plan your trip carefully and seek as much information and prior knowledge as possible, especially from the various motoring organizations.

Australia drives on the left side of the road and displays easily identifiable traffic signs which are internationally known. (There are also some that you won't find anywhere else in the world, such as "Kangaroos for the next 15 km" or "Wombats Crossing".) The speed limits are in kilometers per hour and petrol is sold in liters.

Competition exists among the petrol

stations and most display their prices prominently in the forecourt. It is sometimes possible to save several cents a liter if you keep an alert eye open for a good price.

Traffic rules are common throughout the country, but if you are in any doubt contact the state motoring organization. Each State has its own motoring organization, which will help you with information and arrangements, as well as providing an emergency roadside service. These are:

Adelaide, Royal Automobile Association of South Australia, 41 Hindmarsh Square. Tel: (08) 2234555.

Brisbane, Royal Automobile Club of Queensland, 190 Edward Street. Tel: (07) 2532444.

Canberra, National Roads and Motorists Association, 92 Northbourne Avenue. Tel: (062) 433777.

Darwin, Automobile Association of the Northern Territory, 79 Smith Street. Tel: (089) 813837.

Hobart, Royal Automobile Club of Tasmania, Murray Streets. Tel: (002) 346611.

Melbourne, Royal Automobile Club of Victoria, 123 Queens Street. Tel: (03) 697 2211.

Perth, Royal Automobile of Western Australia 228 Adelaide Terrace. Tel: (09) 325 0551.

Sydney, NRMA, 151 Clarence Street. Tel: (02) 260 9222.

TAXIS

Cabs cruising for hire display a lighted Vacant sign on the roof. There is a set amount for flag fall and then a charge for every part of a kilometer. A surcharge is added for a booked call. Drivers do not expect a tip fixed upon a percentage of the fare, but it is normal to leave the small change of maybe 20 or 30 cents.

ACCOMMODATION

Your choice is from the super five-star hotel to the humble country pub. In the former you can expect international-class service, in the latter the facilities

BELOW Goldrush ostentation of a Kalgoorlie hotel.

and accommodation will vary enormously, but you will get an opportunity to meet some of the locals and be told an unlikely tale or two.

HOTELS

All the State capitals and Canberra have top-class international-standard hotels, with Hiltons to be found in Sydney, Melbourne, Perth, Brisbane and Adelaide and Sheratons in Sydney, Melbourne, Brisbane, Adelaide and Perth. The minimum room rate in a five-star hotel is about $100 a day. The most expensive hotel is The Regent in Sydney where a suite can cost up to $1,000 a day. Australia's biggest hotel is the 659-room Conrad International on Queensland's Gold Coast, which incorporates Jupiter's Casino. Most of the hotel groups have a reservations system through which bookings can be made nation-wide and sometimes overseas depending on the international associations of the hotel. If you stay for a week or more you will probably qualify for a discount, and there are usually attractive weekend packages or family rates.

MOTELS

Considering Australia's dependence on the car it is not surprising that the backbone of the accommodation business is the motel, many hundreds of which stretch across the continent. Again they extend from the luxurious to the budget-basic, with those at the top of the range providing all the comforts of a leading hotel, including spas and saunas. At a top motel you can expect to pay close to $100 a day, and maybe even more.

An average motel is clean and comfortable, with air-conditioning, television and radio and that particularly Australian convenience, an electric water jug and everything you need to make a cup of coffee or tea. There is also likely to be a swimming pool. A light or a full breakfast is available, and it is more than likely that the dining room will serve dinner, or at least on weekdays.

However, weekends might be a different story. Under Australian law, employers must pay their workers higher wages for weekend work, and as many owners feel this is not financially worthwhile they don't bother to open. If you run into this problem, get the motel to recommend a local restaurant. The average motel works out at about $35-$50 a night, room only. Flag and Homestead are the two biggest chains, with about 400 premises each.

COUNTRY PUBS AND FARMS

The country pub can be something of a gamble. The growth of motels has allowed publicans to get out of the habit of putting up overnight guests. Many pubs do not have air-conditioning or private bathrooms, so you might have to make some sacrifices in your efforts to soak up the local color. People eat early in the country, so make sure you dine before the shutters come down. What you may lose in the evening you will likely make up for the next morning - hearty breakfasts are the norm in pubs.

Some farm properties take in paying guests, putting them up in the homestead or in shearers' sheds or bunkhouses. A list of these properties can be obtained from the State tourism organizations. In Tasmania a number of farmers and owners of small cottages and historic colonial houses have formed an association to take in guests. Some of the cottages are in Hobart's Battery Point, a delightful scenic spot.

YOUTH HOSTELS

More than 130 youth hostels are spread across the country, providing the inexpensive accommodation and friendly

company found in youth hostels the world over. Costs are kept to a minimum by asking hostellers to share the jobs. The Australian YHA is affiliated with the International YHA and there is an office in every State.

They can be found at:

New South Wales, 355 Kent Street, Sydney. Tel: (02) 295068.

Northern Territory, Darwin Hostel Complex, Beton Road, Berrimah. Tel: (089) 843902.

Queensland, 462 Queen Street, Brisbane. Tel: (07) 221 2022.

South Australia, Recreation and Sports Center, King and Sturt streets, Adelaide. Tel: (08) 515583.

Tasmania, 133A Elizabeth Street, Hobart. Tel: (002) 349617.

Victoria, 233 Flinders Street, Melbourne. Tel: (03) 635421.

Western Australia, 257 Adelaide Terrace, Perth. Tel: (09) 325 5844.

TOURIST INFORMATION

Each State has its own tourism department, with headquarters in the capital city (see the appropriate chapter on each State for details). These offices are staffed with experienced and extremely helpful personnel (some of whom speak foreign languages) who will supply you with maps and leaflets and help with travel plans.

An interstate network also means that every State is represented in almost every other State. In addition, international visitors can obtain information from the **Australian Tourist Commission**, 324 Street Kilda Road, Melbourne, Victoria 3004. Tel: (03) 690 3900.

Various mini-guides detailing information on specific areas or fields will help you get the most out of your visit. Tasmania's tourism department publishes an excellent series of *"Let's Talk About..."* brochures, New South Wales has its *"Find Yourself or Lose Yourself"* series of guides, while Western Australia publishes a holiday *"WA Guide"* series. The Northern Territory Tourism Commission has produced a number of high-quality publications. The Australian Tourism Commission publishes the very useful book, *"Fare Go,"* full of details covering the entire continent.

The State organizations also operate regional offices in the most popular holiday destination areas, and local councils can often provide literature and information on the immediate area. Look for the sign of a big white "i" on a blue background designating an information office. Local council offices are open weekdays during office hours. If there is no council office in a town, a shopkeeper will often act as the tourism representative so just ask around.

If you have a particular sport or hobby and wish to devote some time to it, the tourism departments can point you in the right direction. Visits or tours can be arranged for gliding, white-water raft-

---

ABOVE A Brisbane church has been converted to a pancake house, complete with medieval atmosphere.

ing, hang gliding, beachcombing, diving, prospecting, factory visits, backpacking and day walks, vineyard tours and bird watching.

NATIONAL PARKS

Australia has several hundred national parks, ranging in size from entire deserts and mountain ranges to small pockets of land which contain some facet of natural significance. As well as being established to protect the natural scenic beauty, other parks exist to guard rare animals or birds.

The establishment and operation of the parks are the responsibility of the State governments, national parks and wildlife services, who provide brochures and details of the facilities at parks. The services are:

New South Wales 189-193 Kent Street, Sydney 2000. Tel: (02) 237 6500.
Queensland, 239 George Street, Brisbane 4000. Tel: (07) 227 4111.
Tasmania, 16 Magnet Court, Sandy Bay 7005. Tel: (002) 308033.
South Australia, 55 Grenfell Street, Adelaide 5000. Tel: (08) 216 7777.
Victoria, 240 Victoria Parade, East Melbourne 3022. Tel: (03) 651 4011.
Western Australia, Hackett Drive, Crawley 6099. Tel: (09) 386 8811.
Northern Territory, Gap Road, Alice Springs. Tel: (089) 508211.

WEIGHTS AND MEASURES

All measures are metric. If you are not used to this method, here are a few approximate equivalents: one kilogram equals two pounds; four liters equals a gallon; a kilometer is five eighths of a mile; 20°C equals 68°F, 25°C equals 77°F, 30°C equals 85°F; a yard equals a meter.

OPPOSITE Houseboating on the Myall Lakes, near Newcastle.

HEALTH

The wisest move is to arrange health and accident insurance before you arrive in Australia. If you sign up once you land, you could find a waiting period before any claims can be made. And it might also be worthwhile including dental insurance in the policy. Hospitals are well-equipped with highly-trained staff, but a visit could prove expensive - as could a call on a doctor.

Drug stores are staffed by qualified pharmacists, and cities have all-night rosters for emergencies. A simple inquiry will help you find the local general practitioner.

CLOTHING

With the wide range of climates in the country at any given time, it is advisable to bring both hot and cold weather clothing. Even if you come in the height of summer, it can occasionally be cool in the southeast mainland States, while in Tasmania and during nights in the inland it can be chilly at any time of the year. A warm sweater or jacket will never go amiss. During winter in the southeast States an overcoat or raincoat and warm clothing are strongly advised.

During summer in the north and center you will need nothing but the lightest of clothing. Shorts are acceptable for men, and are smartened up when worn with long socks. If you intend to be in the sun for any length of time, don't forget to take sunglasses and suntan lotion. Maximum-strength sunscreen lotion is essential if you go out on the water during summer.

Australians tend to dress casually when going out for the evening, proving that it is possible to look casually smart without being scruffy. Gentlemen can generally get into the smartest venues without a tie, although they are expected to wear a jacket. Ladies dress to suit the formality of the occasion.

among the most sought-after duty-free items, but also worth considering are woolen goods and Aboriginal artifacts.

SHOPPING

Foreign visitors are allowed duty-free concessions on a variety of articles, including cameras, electrical equipment and jewelry. A number of shops in the cities specialize in duty free shopping and the discount you receive

COMMUNICATIONS

POST

Post offices are open only during weekdays 9 am to 5 pm, but they will hold mail for visitors. Air-letters cost 45 cents, while postal charges for

will depend on which shop you patronize, so shop around and compare prices.

The travel bureau, your hotel or the Yellow Pages telephone book under "Duty Free" will tell you where to find the shops. Take your passport along, and keep all the paperwork as you will need to present it to Customs when leaving the country.

Opals and other gemstones are

postcards vary, depending on destination. An airmail postcard to the United States costs 50 cents, and one to Britain 55 cents. Some news agents sell stamps, but they do not have the scales to weigh overseas mail and are unlikely to have a list of mailing charges. In these cases, if you are sending overseas mail it is advisable to stick on stamps to a higher value than you estimate necessary, and hope for the best.

TELEPHONES

Phones are found in most hotel and motel rooms, and public call boxes are fairly common. Public phones take 10¢ and 50¢ coins. Local calls cost 30¢ for an unlimited time. Long-distance STD (Subscriber Trunk Dialing) calls can also be made from public boxes and are cheaper after 6 pm and on Sundays. International calls cost just over $6 for a three-minute minimum and then just over $2 for each subsequent minute. You will find international call boxes at airports and city post offices. If you need assistance dial 012 for national inquiries and 0102 for international inquiries.

There is also a system of red and golden phones, found in public places such as hotels and shops. Local and STD calls can be made on these instruments, and some of the gold phones are equipped for international calls. A feature of the golden phone is the digital read-out which shows you how much you have put into the machine, winds down during the call, and indicates when you need to insert more money.

Numbers throughout this book also give you (in brackets) the district prefix, which you omit for local calls. The nation-wide emergency number to call the police, fire service or ambulance is 000.

NEWSPAPERS

Australia has only one national newspaper, *The Australian*, but interstate newspapers are available in leading hotels and news agents on the day of publication. Each State capital has its own morning and evening newspaper, and towards the end of the week they publish supplements containing information such as entertainment and dining-out columns. A number of foreign-language magazines and newspapers are also published in Sydney and Melbourne.

TELEVISION

Five channels are screened in major cities; three commercial outlets and the Australian Broadcasting Corporation (ABC) and SBS. The commercials' overseas material comes mainly from America, while the ABC obtains most of its overseas content from Britain. Program details are found in local newspapers.

EMBASSIES

The telephone numbers of the foreign embassies and High Commissions in Canberra are:
Argentina (062) 951570
Austria (062) 951533
Bangladesh (062) 952155
Belgium (062) 732501
Brazil (062) 731208
Britain (062) 730422
Burma (062) 732753
Canada (062) 733844
Chile (062) 959192
China (062) 412446
Cyprus (062) 952120
Denmark (062) 732195
East Germany (062) 862300
Egypt (062) 950394
European Community (062) 955000
Finland (062) 738000
France (062) 951000
Greece (062) 733011
India (062) 733999
Indonesia (062) 733222
Iran (062) 952544
Iraq (062) 861333
Ireland (062) 733022
Israel (062) 731309
Italy (062) 733333
Japan (062) 733244
Jordan (062) 959951
Kenya (062) 951326
Lebanon (062) 957378
Malaysia (062) 731543
Mauritius (062) 811203
Mexico (062) 733963

Netherlands (062) 733111
New Zealand (062) 7336111
Nigeria (062) 731028
Norway (062) 733444
Pakistan (062) 950021
Papua New Guinea (062) 733322
Peru (062) 951016
Philippines (062) 732535
Poland (062) 731208
Portugal (062) 959992
Singapore (062) 733944
South Africa (062) 732424
South Korea (062) 733044
Soviet Union (062) 959033

Melbourne, (03) 602 1877
Sydney, (02) 277521

Canada:
Brisbane, (07) 231 6522
Melbourne, (03) 654 1433
Sydney, (02) 231 6522

Japan:
Brisbane, (07) 311438
Melbourne, (03) 267 3244
Sydney, (02) 231 3455

New Zealand:
Brisbane, (07) 221 3316
Melbourne, (03) 678111
Sydney, (02) 267 3700

United States:
Brisbane, (07) 839 8955
Melbourne, (03) 699 2244
Sydney, (02) 264 7044

RELIGION

Australia follows the various Christian faiths, predominantly Church of England and Roman Catholic, but the arrival of migrants over the years has also seen the establishment of the Muslim religion in the major cities and there is even the occasional Sikh temple. There are sizable Jewish communities in Sydney and Melbourne.

Details of the services of Christian denominations can be found in Saturday newspapers across the country, not only in the big city journals but also in the local suburban and country papers.

Details of Synagogue services may be obtained by telephoning the Board of Deputies (02) 331 3419 in Sydney, (03) 663 5755 in Melbourne or the Australian Jewish Newspaper, (02) 333 0591.

Spain (062) 733555
Sweden (062) 733033
Switzerland (062) 733977
Thailand (062) 731149
Turkey (062) 950227
Uganda (062) 472236
United States (062) 733711
Uruguay (062) 824418
Vatican (062) 953876
Vietnam (062) 866059
West Germany (062) 733177
Yugoslavia (062) 951458
Zambia (062) 472088

Consuls can be contacted at:
Britain:
Brisbane, (07) 221 4933

ABOVE Shopping in a mall in Newcastle. Large traffic-free shopping centers have sprung up across the country in recent years.

EASY STRINE: AUSTRALIAN SLANG

If you think the locals talk funny, just remember that they probably also find your speech a little strange. However, you will find that a "G'day" (Good Day) will go a long way to cementing a friendship.

Features of Australian words and phrases are rhyming slang and a certain laconic wit such as feeling "crook as Rookwood". ("Crook" means unwell and Rookwood is a Sydney cemetery).

Here are some common terms of Strine or slang Australian just to make you feel at home.

arvo	afternoon
the Alice	Alice Springs
back o' Bourke	far out in the Outback
barbie	barbecue
beaut	excellent
bikie	motorcycle rider
billy	can for boiling tea water
bloke	man
bloody	universal oath
bludger	scrounger
blue	a fight
bookie	bookmaker
bush	anywhere which isn't in the cities or towns
chips	french fries
chook	chicken
chunder	vomit
cobber	friend
crissie	Christmas
cuppa	cup of tea
deli	delicatessen
dingo	wild dog, also a severe insult
dinkum	the truth
dinky di	genuine
dunny	toilet
flog	sell
footy	football
g'day	good day
galah	idiot
get stung	overcharged
grog	alcohol
heart starter	first drink of the day
kick	pocket or wallet
kip	sleep
Kiwi	New Zealander
knocker	critic
knuckle sandwich	a punch
larrikin	hooligan
lob	arrive
loo	toilet
lousy	mean, feeling unwell
lurk	a racket
mate	a good friend
Mick	Roman Catholic
middy	measure of beer
mozzie	mosquito
mug	fool
new chum	new migrant
nong	another fool
O.S.	overseas
Oz	Australia or Australian
pie-eyed	drunk
plonk	cheap wine
pokie	slot machine
poofter	homosexual
ripper	terrific
roo	kangaroo
schooner	a larger measure of beer
scungy	dirty, untidy
she'll be right	everything will be all right
she's sweet	as above
Sheila	young woman
shoot through	leave in a hurry
shout	buy the drink
silvertail	rich establishment figure
slats	ribs
station	large farm
stickybeak	a nosey person
stockman	cowboy
stubby	bottle of beer
TAB	legal betting shop (short for Totaliser Agency Board)
tube	can of beer
two-up	gambling game
tucker	food
turps	alcohol
two-pot screamer	someone who cannot hold his or her drink

Further Reading

GEOFFREY BLAINEY, *A Land Half Won*, Sydney, MacMillan, 1980.

Australia: Land of The Southern Cross, Sydney, Child & Henry, 1986.

Benson & Hedges Restaurant Guide, Sydney, JWC Publications, 1982.

Book of Australia, Sydney, Lansdowne Press, 1982.

Explore Australia, Sydney, George Philip & O'Neil Pty Ltd, 1983.

Heritage of Australia: The Illustrated Register of the National Estate, MacMillan, 1981.

DONALD HORNE, *The Australian People: Biography of a Nation*, Sydney, Angus and Robertson, 1972.

Presenting Australia, Sydney, Child & Henry, 1985.

Presenting Australia's National Parks, Sydney, Child & Henry, 1986.

Sydney Explorer, Sydney, Child & Henry, 1985.

Index

Photo Credits

Photos by Geoff Higgins except those listed below.
5 *left* The Stock House/Penny Tweedie. 6 *right* Adina Amsel. 11 The Stock House/Bob Davis. 12 Douglass Baglin. 14-15 The Stock House/David Austen. 26 The Stock House/Penny Tweedie. 27 The Stock House/David Austen. 28 The Stock House/ Bob Davis. 34 The Stock House/D. & J. Heaton. 52 Adina Amsel. 53 The STock House/John Heaton. 55 The Stock House/Robert Gale. 57 The Stock House/ Bob Davis. 58 The Stock House/Dallas Heaton. 58-59 *bottom* The Stock House/Terry Duckham. 61 The Stock House/Dallas Heaton. 62 The Stock House/D. & J. Heaton. 63 The Stock House/Bob Davis. 67 The Stock House/Paul Lloyd. 70 The Stock House/Bob Davis. 84 Australian Picture Library. 87 The Stock House/Bob Davis. 91 The Stock House/D. & J. Heaton. 97 The Stock House/Paul Steel. 101 The Stock House/D. & J. Heaton. 114 The Stock House/P. J. Mackey. 115 The Stock House/Dallas Heaton. 122 *bottom left* The StockHouse/D. & J. Heaton. 124-125 The Stock House/ Robert Gale. 125 *middle right* The Stock House/Robin Smith. 128 The Stock House/D & J. Heaton. 134-135 Douglass Baglin. 135 Australian Picture Library. 141 The Stock House/D. & J. Heaton. 142 The Stock House/Bob Davis. 149 *top right* The Stock House/Paul Lloyd; *bottom right* The Stock House/Penny Tweedie. 153 The Stock House/ Cary Wolinsky. 154-155 Adina Amsel. 156 The Stock House/Cary Wolinsky. 159 The Stock House/ D. & J. Heaton. 161 The Stock House/Paul Steel. 164-167 Adina Amsel. 175 Robert Wilson. 179 The Stock House/P. J. Mackey. 186 Robert Wilson. 189 The Stock House/ David Austen. 190 Douglass Baglin. 191 The Stock House/David Austen. 192 The Stock House/D. & J. Heaton. 196 The Stock House/D & J. Heaton. 198 *top* The Stock Hosue/David Austen; *bottom* Adina Amsel. 199 *top left* Robert Wilson; *bottom left* Adina Amsel. 204 The Stock House/Cary Wolinsky. 207 Adina Amsel. 209 The Stock House/P. J. Mackey. **Back Cover:** Adina Amsel.